# Are We Captives Of History?

Historical Essays on Turkey and Europe

Edgeir Benum
Alf Johansson
Jan-Erik Smilden
Alf Storrud
(eds.)

Tid og Tanke

Unipub forlag – Oslo Academic Press
2007

© Unipub forlag – Oslo Academic Press
and the Editorial staff of Tid & tanke, 2007

ISSN 0809-0505
ISBN 978-82-7477-280-9

*Tid & tanke*
Publication Series of History, IAKH

*Main editor:*
Alf Johansson

For further information, please contact

Unipub forlag – Oslo Academic Press
Phone: + 47 22 85 33 00
Fax: +47 22 85 30 39
E-mail: post@unipub.no

You may order this publication at www.akademika.no

No portion of this book may be copied in violation of copyright law or contrary to agreements with KOPINOR, the interest group for rights holders of creative works in Norway. Any form of unauthorised copying establishes a liability to compensation and confiscation, and is punishable by fine or imprisonment.

Cover and layout by Unipub forlag – Oslo Academic Press
Printed in Norway by AiT e-dit, 2007

Cover illustration: *Fountain in the Seraglio* by Jean François Trichon, 1882.
Fountain from the Topkapı-palace in Constantinople.

# Foreword

This book is the result of a conference held at the University of Oslo in April 2005 on the subject of 'Turkey and Europe – are we captives of history?' The conference was part of the weekly departmental seminar series of the Department of History.

Turkish membership of the European Union is a controversial issue in many member countries. In the present situation, what attitudes concerning the relationship between the two parties are revealing themselves? And how are such attitudes conditioned by historical memory? Our intention with the conference was to shed light on such questions, focusing especially on European images of Turkey and the Turks, as well as on the handling of 'the European problem' in Turkish history. The questions raised will, we think, continue to be of great importance for years to come.

The bulk of the contributions to this book cover the period from the thirteenth century to the present day. They focus on images coming from different regions of Europe: Italy (Mustafa Soykut), the Balkans (Svein Mønnesland) and Scandinavia (Bernt Brendemoen), as well as on the political role of religion in Turkey (Bjørn Olav Utvik), the historical role of Ottoman rule vis-à-vis the Greek population of Cyprus (Jan-Erik Smilden), and Turkish attitudes to European political arrangements (Pınar Tank).

Two articles have been added since the conference. Ann Helene Bolstad Skjelbred writes on images of the Turk in Norway, and Jon Iddeng traces the origins of the East/West controversy from classical times to the Middle Ages.

*

The contributors approach the image of Turkey and the Turks in various ways. In the first essay Jon W. Iddeng addresses the ancient origin of the East/West controversy, and briefly looks at the clashes between East and West, along with the rise and fall of the many cultures and empires of Anatolia and the Levant until the fall of the Byzantine Empire.

*Mustafa Soykut* shows how the image of Islam – as well as that of the 'Turk' – served to define 'Europeanness' as opposed to the 'other', and describes how this image gradually started to change towards the end of the seventeenth century with Ottoman decline.

*Jan-Erik Smilden* describes how the Turks restored the Orthodox Church in Cyprus, and suggests that Cyprus might have been a Catholic island, like Malta today, if the Turkish invasion had not occurred in 1570.

*Svein Mønnesland* focuses on the Ottoman legacy in south-eastern Europe. His essay seeks to determine to what extent it is a reality in the present-day Balkan states, and how this legacy is reflected in attitudes towards present-day Turkey.

*Bernt Brendemoen* sums up the image of the Turks and Turkey as depicted by Scandinavian travellers in Turkey from the seventeenth century to the end of the nineteenth century.

*Ann Helene Bolstad Skjelbred* shows how folklore and folk narratives about the 'snout' – Turks from the 1800s in Norway may be viewed as expressions of social fear, the fear of strangers and of different social groups.

*Bjørn Olav Utvik* reflects upon the current role of religion in Turkish politics and how this relates to Turkey's efforts to gain entry into the European Union.

*Pınar Tank* describes how the construction of Turkey's identity as Western and secular emerges from the interplay between internal and external perceptions, and examines this ambiguous identity as well as the symbolic significance of EU membership for the Turkish secular elite.

We would like to thank the authors for making their contributions available and ready for publication.

Oslo, December 2006


The Editors

# Contents

| | |
|---|---|
| **Foreword** | 3 |
| **Introduction: In the Shadow of 1683**<br>Jan-Erik Smilden | 7 |
| **The Ancient Origin of the East/West Controversy**<br>Jon W. Iddeng | 13 |
| **The Genealogy of the 'Other':**<br>**The Turks, Islam and Europe**<br>Mustafa Soykut | 31 |
| **When the Turks saved the Greek Cypriots**<br>Jan-Erik Smilden | 71 |
| **Turkey seen from Europe's 'Near East', the Balkans**<br>Svein Mønnesland | 83 |
| **The Image of the Turks and Turkey**<br>**as depicted by Scandinavian Travellers**<br>Bernt Brendemoen | 93 |
| **The Turks in Norwegian Legends**<br>Ann Helene Bolstad Skjelbred | 105 |
| **An Islamic Road to Europe?**<br>Bjørn Olav Utvik | 113 |
| **Turkey's Ambiguous Identity:**<br>**The Symbolic Significance of EU Membership**<br>Pınar Tank | 129 |
| **List of Contributors** | 149 |
| **Earlier publications of Tid og Tanke** | 151 |

# Introduction: In the Shadow of 1683

Jan-Erik Smilden

'The Turks at the gates of Vienna' was the title of an editorial in the liberal Austrian weekly magazine *Profil* just a few days before the European Union was to decide whether Turkey should be admitted to member state negotiations in the autumn of 2004. For many Austrians a possible Turkey EU membership was frightening and filled with negative emotions. A kind of collective memory prevailed, that of the 'vicious Turk' from the historical period of the Ottoman Empire.

Ottoman forces tried to conquer Vienna twice, in 1529 and 1683. Both times they failed, but the sieges were felt as a serious threat, not only in Austria, but also in many other parts of Europe. After the Ottoman conquest of large parts of the Balkans, including the bastion of Orthodox Christianity, Constantinople (in 1453), many feared that the Muslim 'Turkish hordes' would rage through the rest of the European soil and occupy what was left of the Christian heartland. Mothers frightened their children by saying that the Turks would come and abduct them if they misbehaved.

In 2004 the Turks were knocking on the door of Europe again, in a 'third invasion' and in numbers of 70 million, nearly all of them Muslims. This time they came with peaceful intentions, but that was not enough to reassure the opponents and sceptics. 'The relief of Vienna in 1683 will have been in vain', declared the outgoing Dutch European commissioner, Frits Bolkestein. He warned of the 'Islamisation of Europe'.

The 'Turco-sceptics' still play an important role in the EU. One thing is Turkeys' treatment of its Kurdish minority and a generally dubious reputation concerning human rights and the freedom of speech, the latter actualised recently when Orhan Pamuk, the winner of the Nobel Prize in literature, faced prosecution because he had said in an interview that a million Armenians were killed by the Turks in 1915.[1] Another thing is the religious aspect, with so many Muslims entering the Christian-dominated union. This fear of Islam seems to be increasing, first and foremost because of the 'war on terror'. In that respect Turkey has been a victim of 9/11. But just as important is the actual scepticism toward the Turks, based on the prevailing historical

---

[1] 'The Armenian Question' is still one of the most controversial subjects in Turkish history.

apprehension. Old prejudices from Ottoman times are re-emerging. History is once again a tool for policy-making.

The Ottoman Empire was one of history's greatest imperial systems, existing from the fourteenth century to 1923, when Mustafa Kemal Atatürk established the Turkish republic. It stretched into most of the Middle East and the Balkans, and we still find the Ottoman imprint in these regions; in culture, language, architecture, traditions – and in history. Today's Turkey is much smaller and less important than the Ottoman Empire, but one must not underestimate the importance of this country, situated in both Europe and Asia, as a bridge-builder between East and West and between Islam and Christianity. In the Middle East, Turkey neighbours Iran, Iraq and Syria, three volatile states with an uncertain future. In the Caucasus it borders the former Soviet republics of Georgia and Armenia and in Europe the EU countries of Bulgaria and Greece. Turkey is a member of NATO and has a defence cooperation agreement with Israel, even though it is now governed by the Islamist-leaning AK-party. The moderate version of Islam practised by the AK leaders differs considerably from the kind of Islamism prevailing in Iran and parts of Iraq.

Turcophobia has its roots in the Crusades when Pope Urban II called upon all Christians to join the war against the Turks in 1095. In the middle of the fifteenth century special masses were arranged in various places in Europe. These anti-Turkish sentiments persisted and were even strengthened when the Ottomans entered the military and political scene. The historical road of the Ottoman Empire is scattered with negative descriptions and stereotypes, such as 'the lustful Turk', 'the grand Turk', 'the sick man of Europe' and 'the Eastern Question'. Marin Luther spoke of the Turks as 'the people of the wrath of God', Christian I, king of Denmark and Norway declared that 'the grand Turk was the monster rising from the sea in the Apocalypse'. The British scholar Andrew Wheatcroft writes that for the Europeans, the Ottoman Empire 'manifested all the negative qualities they associated with the Orient: exoticism, sexual licence, cruelty and deceit.'[2] In November 1914, during the first stages of the First World War, David Lloyd George, the then British Prime Minister, declared: 'The Turks are a human cancer, a creeping agony in the flesh of the lands which they misgovern, rotting every fibre of life… I am glad that the Turk is to be called to a final account for his long record of infamy against humanity.'[3]

Novelists too have had their prejudices, with profound consequences. One good example is the Croat Ivo Andrić, winner of the Nobel Prize in Literature in 1961. His famous book *The Bridge on the Drina* is a fantastic novel, but at the same time full

---

[2] Andrew Wheatcroft, *The Ottomans, dissolving Images* (London: Penguin Books, 1995), p. xxi.
[3] Quoted from a speech by Lloyd George, cited in H.W.V. Temperley (ed.), *A History of the Peace Conference in Paris* (Oxford 1969), VI, 24.

of stereotypical characteristics of the Muslim Turks, hated and despised by many Catholic Croats. On the executions that were carried out on the Drina bridge, Andrić writes: 'The job of headsman was for long always carried out by the same soldier. He was a fat and dark-skinned Anatolian with dull yellowish eyes and negroid lips in a greasy and earthen-coloured face, who seemed always to be smiling, with a smile of a well-nourished and good-humoured man.'[4] In the book a delegate from the sultan in Istanbul is characterised as a 'soft pale fellow from Stamboul', the captain of the guard in Vishegrad is 'a sickly Anatolian', his sergeant Tahir 'an evil man, sullen and rheumy-eyed'.

What is the reason for these negative attitudes towards the Turks throughout history? The Ottomans originated from a Turkish tribe of the Central Asian steppes. The Europeans considered this people as 'barbaric', with a warlike spirit. The 'Turk' was not only 'vicious' and 'bloodthirsty', he was also 'infidel', 'unreliable' and alien, with his different religion, his strange clothes and his odd habits. He was backward both culturally and politically. The leader of the Turk, the sultan was a 'cruel tyrant' who (according to the tales) gorged himself in luxury in his harem of oppressed slave women, sexually insatiable.

Of course the Ottomans were warriors, as many other Europeans were at that time. It is true that they occasionally killed their enemies by putting them on stakes, but we must remember that their European Christian contemporaries burned women accused of witchcraft or threw them into water to see if they floated or not. The sultan could be a tyrant, as other leaders in Europe could be, but there is no way to generalize. Sultan Mehmet II, who conquered Constantinople in 1453 is said to have spoken six languages. Sultan Süleyman the Magnificent was an intellectual and a great patron of artists and philosophers (not least Westerners). He spoke several languages and was a notable poet in Persian. His wife Roxelana[5] (most likely from the Ukraine) was probably the most powerful woman in the whole history of the Ottoman Empire, with a great influence on her husband. Recent research done by Leslie P. Peirce[6] shows that the harem was not an imperial whorehouse, but a political and administrative institution where decisions were made and where women, by wisdom, smartness, manipulation, patience and intrigue, could climb the ladder and obtain enormous power.

The body of research on Ottoman history is growing, and through the study of available sources the stereotypical picture of the quondam Turk is becoming more

---

[4] Ivo Andrić, *The Bridge on the Drina* (trans. L.F. Edwards), (Beograd: Dereta, 2000), p. 91.
[5] Her Turkish name was Hürrem.
[6] Leslie P. Peirce, *The Imperial Harem, Women and Sovereignty in the Ottoman Empire* (New York: Oxford University Press, 1993).

nuanced. There is also important research going on in former Ottoman territories that is correcting the traditional black and white attitudes. In Cyprus for instance, the young Greek Cypriot historian Marios Hadjianastasis has examined aspects of the social and economic history of seventeenth-century Ottoman Cyprus, a century that had remained largely understudied.[7] He finds that the conflict during this period was much more a class struggle than an ethnic or religious conflict. His findings differ considerably from the common understanding found in Greek Cypriot historiography.

Two interesting books on the image of the Turks have been published in Istanbul, based on a conference and a workshop respectively.[8] They give a comprehensive picture of historical and contemporary views on the Ottoman Empire, Turkey and the Turkish people. The Turkish historian Mustafa Soykut, one of the contributors to this volume, did his Ph.D. on studies of Italian sources between 1453 (the fall of Constantinople) and 1683 (the siege of Vienna).[9] By using these original sources, he produced a pioneering work in Ottoman studies.

Recent research also gives a lot of credit to the Ottomans concerning the Renaissance in Europe. *Re-orienting the Renaissance*[10] contains a range of essays from leading scholars and writers which challenge settled certainties about the difference between East and West and Islam and Christianity. The famous writer and historian William Dalrymple writes in the foreword: 'At all levels, the Ottoman world impinged directly on Renaissance life, and the intellectual awakening that the Renaissance represented owed almost as much from the interplay of East and West as it did to any process of self-regeneration drawing from Greek and Roman roots'[11].

In Norway, Iver B. Neumann[12] has an interesting approach. He discusses the 'East' in European identity formation and writes that 'the Turk' remains the dominant other in the history of European state systems.[13] He also discusses whether the Ottoman Empire was considered as a European realm or not. Considering that the Ottoman Empire included a substantial part of Europe, this is a pertinent question.

---

[7] Marios Hadjianastasis, *Bishops, Ağas and Dragomans: A Social and Economic History of Ottoman Cyprus 1640–1704* (Birmingham: School of Historical Studies, University of Birmingham, 2004) (Ph. D. thesis.)

[8] Mustafa Soykut (ed.), *Historical Image of the Turk in Europe: 15th Century to the present* (Istanbul: The Isis Press, 2003), and Nedret Kuran Borçoğlu (ed.), *The Image of the Turk in Europe from the Declaration of the Republic 1923 to the 1990s* (Istanbul: The Isis Press, 2000).

[9] Mustafa Soykut, *Image of the 'Turk' in Italy* (Berlin: Klaus Schwarz Verlag, 2001).

[10] Gerald MacLean (ed.), *Re-orienting the renaissance, Cultural Exchanges with the East* (Basingstoke, Hampshire: Palgrave Macmillan, 2005).

[11] Ibid, p. xv

[12] Iver B. Neumann, *Uses of the Other: 'The East in European Identity Formation'* (Minneapolis: University of Minnesota, 1999).

[13] Neumann, p. 39.

In an historical context it is also interesting to discuss the concepts of 'Turk' and 'Ottoman'. The Europeans mostly used 'Turk', which in many ways became a term of abuse and a description of a feared and hated enemy. Paradoxically this word did not have a positive nuance in Istanbul either. The rulers in the Ottoman capital called themselves 'Ottomans', heirs of Osman, the founder of the empire. 'Turk' was originally a description of the Turkmen nomads from Anatolia where Osman's tribe, the Oğuz, was one among others. According to Mustafa Soykut the 'Turks' were looked upon as primitive and brutal and not a part of the Ottoman elite.[14] When people from the upper classes in Istanbul used the word 'Turk' it was often a derogatory term, referring to a farmer from Anatolia.

In reality Europe and Turkey have a common history, not least during the Ottoman period. There is a common heritage that one will discover, not least in the Balkans, in Greece and in Cyprus. One will find it in the language, in the food, in the architecture, and often in the culture in general. But this common heritage is not always uncontroversial. The starch and sugar-made sweet Turkish Delight, is a favourite among Greek Cypriots, but in Greek Cyprus it is called 'Cyprus Delight'. To use the Turkish version is not recommended on that side of the island.

In Muslim parts of the Balkans one will still today find many traces of the Ottomans, not only in mosques and tekkes,[15] but also in house construction and not least in memory. The town of Prizren in Kosovo is still dominated by its Ottoman past, both in appearance and in spirit. Many of the coffee shops have their televisions tuned into Turkish stations rather than the local ones, Turkish football is popular, and many people have relatives in Turkey. During the Cold War, when Kosovo was a part of communist Yugoslavia, there was a bus service once a week from Prizren to Istanbul in NATO-aligned Turkey.

Our intention in publishing this volume is to give a broader understanding of the Turks' relations to the rest of the European countries, for it is an indisputable fact that Turkey is a part of Europe. The contributors are Turkish as well as Norwegian scholars. They present historical as well as contemporary approaches.

Are we captives of history? That is the question we are asking, and to a certain extent the answer is affirmative. The question is also, as I write in my own essay, who has won the war on history in this part of the world? That is definitely not the Turks. But it remains to be seen if Turkey will win the fight against the 'Turco-sceptics' in the European Union and become a fully-fledged member state.

---

[14] Soykut (2001).
[15] A lodge of a dervish order, a centre of worship.

# The Ancient Origin of the East/West Controversy

Jon W. Iddeng

It is a truism that the Middle East is the cradle of human civilisation, but also that classical Greece is the cradle of Western civilisation. What can be made of this, besides the fact that we all were once infants (and some of us apparently twice)? When and how did Greece become a cradle of its own, a symbol of Europe and the West, in opposition to the older civilisations in the Middle East? What constituted the difference between East and West before the coming of Islam and the Ottoman Empire?

This essay will address the ancient origin of the East/West controversy in times long before the Turks appeared on the stage, and briefly look at the clashes between East and West along with the rise and fall of the many cultures and empires of Anatolia and the Levant until the fall of the Byzantine Empire.

## Greece, Anatolia and the Middle East until the End of the Bronze Age

Anatolia can, with Çatalhöyük, claim to contain one of the oldest cities in the world (probably only beaten by Jericho) and the Karacadag Mountains still host wild einkorn, and may have been where the cultivation of wheat began. So there can be little doubt that parts of what is present day Turkey were among the very first human settlements. The spread of Indo-European languages suggests migration and connections between Asia and Europe, with Asia Minor as the bridge. Linguists and archaeologists have discovered traces of non-Indo-European languages and culture in several places around the Aegean basin, and have made the case for a migration of a non-Indo-European people from Asia Minor to the islands and Greek mainland some time during the fourth century BCE. For convenience these people have been called 'Pelasgians', as both Homer and Herodotus describe a non-Greek indigenous people of the Aegean with the name *Pelasgoi*.[1]

It is, however, the Fertile Crescent that is credited with giving birth to the first complex societies or civilisations, the river valley civilisations; the first Sumerian city states, the later Akkadian empire in Mesopotamia and the old kingdom in Egypt. By the time of the Bronze Age, however, the whole of the Middle East and the Eastern Mediterranean consisted of, or was more or less controlled by, complex civilisations. The mythical king Minos of Crete was the first to organise a navy according to Greek legend (Thucydides 1.4; 1.8), and it seems probable that Crete was a centre of the East Mediterranean palace culture of the mid Bronze Age, controlling the Cyclades and Aegean islands. Remains of early Bronze Age societies are moreover found in several places in various parts of Anatolia, in what was called the land of the Hatti in Akkadian sources.

The first large empire to appear with a base in Anatolia was the kingdom of the Hittites, expanding from the capital Hattuša (present Boghazköy) in the seventeenth century BCE. At the height of its power in the fourteenth and thirteenth century, the Hittite empire included large areas in Anatolia and the Levant, from the Aegean to the Euphrates. When excavations began in Boghazköy, archaeologists found a rich corpus of texts written in cuneiform, including several treaties in Akkadian with foreign powers from Egypt to the neighbouring Mitanni. We can read about contacts, trade and strife between these highly developed Bronze Age cultures of the southeastern Mediterranean and Mesopotamia, including that which has been identified as Mycenaean.[2] Even Cyprus (Alašiya) was conquered and claimed as part of the Hittite empire. The records tell of King Shuppiluliuma II's successful campaign in the early twelfth century, but also of mighty warriors 'who live in ships', settling on the Anatolian coast. Archaeological evidence suggests that there was also frequent contact and trade with palaces of the prevailing Mycenaean culture to the west and further east towards the Indus.[3] We can conclude that the Hittites were in the midst of a highly developed Bronze Age palace culture, with contact and commerce across

---

[1] Cf. R. Drews, *The Coming of the Greeks: Indo-European Conquests in the Aegean and the Near East* (Princeton, N.J.: Princeton University Press, 1988).
[2] T. Bryce, *The Kingdom of the Hittites* (Oxford: Oxford University Press, 1998).
[3] See for instance Ian Morris, *Archaeology as Cultural History* (2000), J. Hooker, *Mycenaean Greece* (1977) and P.A. Mountjoy, 'The East Aegean-West Anatolian interface in the Late Bronze Age: Mycenaeans and the Kingdom of Ahhiyawa', *AS* 48 (1998), pp. 33-67.

enormous distances of the Eurasian continent, in what scholars today call a Near Eastern and Aegean cultural community (*koinê*).[4]

The collapse of these Bronze Age cultures at the end of the thirteenth century is still something of a puzzle, and many attempts have been made to explain it, such as volcanic eruptions, floods and a breakdown in trade patterns. Archaeological findings indicate a migration of Bronze Age warlords eastwards as the Mycenaean palace civilisations crumpled and there are Egyptian sources describing the attack of the 'Sea Peoples' who destroyed the Hittite empire and many other states during the reigns of Merneptah (c. 1220 BCE) and Rameses III (c. 1185 BCE). We will never be certain about the nature of the 'Sea Peoples', but most agree that they comprise different peoples from several places and that they came from somewhere in the north, and thus (interestingly given our present concern) may be an early instance of 'European' raids on the Middle East.[5] One of the groups mentioned in the Egyptian records, the *Peleset*, seems to have been absorbed into the Egyptian military service, and they are commonly identified with the *Philistines*, and it is probable that they by and large gained control over the Egyptian possessions in the southern Levant, organising independent cities when the Egyptians no longer managed to control the Canaanite area around 1150 BCE. *Peleset* is also similar to *Pelasgoi*, which, as we have seen is used by Greek sources to describe aboriginal people of the Aegean, but also connected to *pelagos* (Greek for 'open sea'), thus also connecting them with some sort of seafarers.[6] It is also tempting to link this to the Biblical story (Deut. 2.23) of invaders from Caphtor to the Gaza area. The Caphtorim have been connected to Crete or Cyprus, so perhaps the Philistines with their five-city (*pentapolis*) stronghold were early invaders from the Aegean islands to the Levant. Yet all traces

---

[4] W. Burkert, *The Orientalizing Revolution* (1992), idem 'Near Eastern connections' in *A Companion to Ancient Epic*, (Foley ed., 2005), pp. 291-301. See also A. Kuhrt, *The Ancient Near East c. 3000-330 BCE* (2 vols, 1995) and M.H. Feldman, *Diplomacy by Design: Luxury Arts and an 'International Style' in the Ancient Near East, 1400-1200 BCEE* (2006).
[5] Cf. E.D. Oren (ed.), *The Sea Peoples and Their World: A Reassessment* (Philadelphia, 2000) for an updated review of the question.
[6] Herodotus 1.56-58. In *Iliad* the Pelasgians are allies of Troy, standing between the Hellespontine cities and the Thracians in the Catalogue of Ships (2.840-843). The *Odyssey* (17.175-177) places the Pelasgians in Crete, but in Homer and Herodotus the term 'Pelasgian' is usually synonymous with 'ancient times', 'Greece before the Greeks' etc. See e.g. A.M. Biraschi, 'Kreston huper Tursenon: a proposito di Hdt. I 57: mito e tradizione storiografica', *GeogrAnt* 5 (1996), pp. 163-169.

of a non-Semitic language and a distinct foreign culture are gone, so if this was the case, they were very quick to adapt to Canaanite culture.[7]

The so-called Dark Age following the collapse of the palace civilisations (c. 1100-800 BCE) is not completely dark anymore, but remains misty. Whereas empires and monarchies were established again in the Middle East and Asia Minor, Greece went from palace to polis. It was a shift from relatively few but large settlements, to many and small ones. What emerged was not the first city-state culture in the history of mankind, as city-states had appeared in Mesopotamia and particularly in the Levant from the early Sumerians to the Phoenicians, but it was the largest.[8] What was particular about the evolution of the Greek city-states, however, was their egalitarian political structure, with the communities being organised around a body of citizens with political and juridical rights. This has been described as something unique, 'a political revolution', in the words of the leading German historian Christian Meier, who claims that 'we may see the Greeks as a needle's eye through which world history had to pass in order to reach the stage of European and worldwide modernity.'[9]

The Near Eastern influence on Greek culture is by now firmly established, and will no doubt continue to be explored and demonstrated by further studies.[10] This does not, of course, mean that the Greek contribution to later thought and society is insignificant, but the uniqueness of Greek political awareness and rationality is beginning to be questioned. What is of importance to our present concern is nevertheless that the Greeks and the Greek city-state culture did not arise in a Dark Age void. They were inspired and affected by Near Eastern societies, not doubting that *ex oriente lux*. After all, Europa was a beautiful young girl abducted by Zeus from the shores of the Middle East, according to Greek myth.

The Greeks colonised large stretches of the shores of the Mediterranean and the Black Sea, including the islands of the Aegean and the coast of Asia Minor from c. 1000 BCE onwards, but we know very little of how these societies were organised.

---

[7] On the ancient Philistines, see J. Strange, *Caphtor-Keftiu. A new investigation* (1980), idem 'The Philistine city-states', in M.H. Hansen (ed.) *A Comparative Study of Thirty City-State Culture* (2000), pp. 129-139, I. Vincentelli,'Appunti sulle nuove proposte di localizzazione di Caphtor/Keftiw', *SMEA* 24 (1984), pp. 263-267, and M. Delcor, 'Les Kerethim et les Crétois', *VT* 28 (1978), pp. 409-422.

[8] Cf. M.H. Hansen, *A Comparative Study of Thirty City-State Culture* (2000).

[9] C. Meier, 'The Greeks: The political revolution in world history' [orig.1982], in P.J. Rhodes (ed.), *Athenian Democracy* (Oxford: Oxford University Press, 2004), p. 330.

[10] Here shall only be mentioned three momentous works, Martin Bernal, *Black Athena: The Afroasiatic Roots of Classical Civilisation* (London: Free Association Books, 1987); Walter Burkert, *The Orientalizing Revolution: Near Eastern influence on Greek Culture in Early Archaic Age* (Cambridge, Mass.: Harvard University Press, 1992) and Martin L. West, *The East Face of Helicon* (Oxford: Clarendon Press, 1997). Cf. also K. Dowden, 'West on the East: Martin West's "East face of Helicon" and its forerunners', in *JHS* 121 (2001), pp. 167-175.

When they appear in our sources some hundred years later the Greek 'colonies' form a network of city-states dominating parts of the coastline of Asia Minor. The world that emerges in archaic times is one of an expanding Greek culture, settling alongside foreign cities and powers, such as Phoenician city-states on Cyprus, the Egyptian kingdom in the Nile delta and the kingdoms of large inland territories, such as Phrygia, Lydia and Caria. Naturally, they did not always live in peace and harmony, but there was apparently no strife between East and West, and the Hellespont and Bosporus did not form a border area separating West/Europe from East/Asia.

Still, arguably the most famous of all ancient battles was fought out between the Greek West and the non-Greek East some time in the golden age of the palaces, and put on record in archaic Greek times: *The Trojan War*. An overwhelming number of scholars have contributed to the debate on Homer, the Homeric question, Homeric societies and language and so on, and whether or not a Trojan War was ever fought.[11] The excavated palace(s) in Hissarlık, first found by the adventurous German Heinrich Schliemann in the 1880s, fits well with a characteristic Bronze Age palace such as Troy would have been, but can hardly be identified with Priam's great kingdom. Yet archaeological findings and Hittite texts suggest a period of strife and attacks in Hissarlık-Troy during the thirteenth century, attacks that may well have been carried out by Mycenaeans, even if Troy was never of any great importance in Anatolian history and did not vanish as a result of this onslaught.[12]

What is of great relevance to our present concern is the fact that even if this war is depicted as one between all Greeks against Troy and their non-Greek allies, Homer never creates an us-and-them picture of good guys and bad guys. It is a tale with heroes and humans on both sides, tragically and inevitably fighting a war caused by divine quarrel, with the gods divided in their support of the combatants as well. Homer uses the word 'barbarian' rarely, and only in the sense of 'not Greek-speaking'. Much the same can be said of other extant poets of Greek archaic times, such as Hesiod and Alcaeus. In Greek myth there were also other instances of Greek skirmishes with the east, such as battles with Amazons and the expedition of Jason and the Argonauts, but it seems safe to conclude that the Greek West had no major quarrel with the non-Greek East before the mid-sixth century BCE.

---

[11] Cf. B. Powell, *Homer* (Oxford, 2003), for an update on various topics.
[12] Recent overviews of Troy and the possible historicity of the Trojan war can be found in T. Bryce, *The Kingdom of the Hittites* (Oxford: Oxford University Press, 1998), pp. 392-404 and J. Lactaz, *Troy and Homer* (Oxford: Oxford University Press, 2004).

Jon W. Iddeng

# Greeks and Persians in Classical Times

Homer's *Iliad* stands at the beginning of a new epoch of writing, as in all probability it was the first major literary text written in the newly developed Greek alphabet. The Greek alphabet was, however, no Western innovation, but borrowed and adapted from the Semitic alphabet of the Phoenicians. The Greeks soon developed a written culture, as not only administrative records and treaties were set down on clay or metal plates, but papyrus was used to record and circulate songs, epic tales, plays and various kinds of prose narratives. They produced written investigations [*historiē*] of the world, its peoples and their past. The first recognised historian, Herodotus, deals with the crucial war at the beginning of classical Greek times, but tells many stories of people, kings and empires interacting with the Greek world in what we label 'archaic' times (800-500 BCE).[13] We learn about generations of Lydian kings, the whole of the second book of his work is devoted to Egypt, and other more or less civilised people Greeks were visiting, dealing with, fighting against, being mercenaries for or hiring as mercenaries. Yet something has changed from Homer, which is evident in the writings of the rather cosmopolitan historian from Halicarnassus in Asia Minor: the Greeks had developed an ideology of themselves as unique and superior to all other mankind, who were barbarians, *barbaroi*. This is evident in much of our extant Greek literature from classical times (c. 500-300 BCE). What had happened?

The Persians had entered the stage. After centuries of Greek expansion and progress, with colonies (*apoikiai*) and trading places (*emporia*) all around the Mediterranean and Black Sea, they had suddenly met with an enemy that threatened not only the odd city on foreign soil, but Greece proper. From its base in Fars in present day Iran, the Persians had built an empire larger than any other in the known world under their famous king Cyrus (558-530 BCE). The Persian Empire expanded in all directions and included the Hindu Kush and the west bank of the Indus river in the southeast, the Caucasus and, after beating the legendary King Croesus of Lydia in the mid-540s, Anatolia in the northeast. Soon after, the neo-Babylonian empire was subjugated and the Persians gained control of all Mesopotamia and the Levant. Persian rule was by no means a regime of terror as, for instance, that of the Assyrians had been, and both their culture and government were sophisticated. Their rule was based on local and provincial administration (*satrapies*) and tribute in the form of taxes measured out in silver.

---

[13] On Herodotus and his world view, cf. R.Thomas, *Herodotus in Context: Ethnography, Science and the Art of Persuasion* (Cambridge, U.K., New York: Cambridge University Press, 2000), R. Bichler, *Herotots Welt: Der Aufbau der Historie am Bild der fremden Länder und Völker, ihrer Zivilisation und ihrer Geschichte* (2000) and C.B.R. Pelling, 'East is east and west is west: or are they? National stereotypes in Herodotus', *Histos* (1997).

## The Ancient Origin of the East/West Controversy

After Cyrus's death his son Cambyses continued the conquest, and by 525 BCE Egypt was conquered, and Herodotus outlines how Greeks fought as mercenaries on both sides. It was, however the next king Darius (521-486) who would cause the Greeks serious problems. The Greek city-states of the Asian coast had for some time been subject to Lydia, but the Persians wanted a firmer grip on them and even subdued the islands near the coast on their way. In 500 BCE the Ionian Greeks united in a revolt, and although the support from the other Greeks was sparse, the Athenians sent a small fleet to their aid. Darius repressed the rebellion and made sure to eliminate the tyrants of the Ionian cities and replace them with democratic institutions on the way, if Herodotus (6.43) can be trusted on this issue. The Persians also crossed the Hellespont and entered Europe, subduing Thrace and Macedonia. In 490 BCE they launched the well-known attack on Greece and the Athenians, but were beaten at the legendary battle of Marathon; ten years later they returned with an even larger force and a new king, Xerxes. But yet again the Greeks managed to win the decisive battles, and what was left of the Persian troops had to return and the nearly all the Greek city-states of Asia Minor were freed from Persian rule. These famous 'Persian Wars' are significant in Greek history and crucial for the development of a Greek pan-Hellenic and anti-Oriental mentality.[14] The fact that they have entered our history as the *Persian* Wars illustrates the point of a European discourse of *us and them* ever since.[15]

Persia was for obvious reasons considered a threat to Greek interests at the beginning of classical times, and the Greeks realised the need to unite not just in arms, but also in words. An anti-Persian discourse or propaganda was developed. After 479 BCE the Greeks became all the more attentive to their own superiority and the Persians were stereotyped and monarchic rule vilified. Denigrating the enemy was certainly nothing new at the time, but the fact that it was put down in writing, in literary texts and treaties to be passed along from generation to generation for later laymen and scholars to read, was decisive.

Aeschylus entered the drama contest of the Dionysus festival in 472 BCE with the play *Persians*, and here the new trend is made clear. Here the Persian messenger brings the Greek war slogan to the court at Susa: 'Forward, sons of the Greeks, liberate the fatherland, liberate your children, your women, the temples of your ancestral gods, the graves of your forebears: this is the battle for everything!'[16] And the chorus later gives the happy state of affairs for the Greeks: 'No longer will tongues in vassal

---
[14] Cf. Paul Cartledge, *The Greeks* (Oxford: Oxford University Press, 1993) and *Thermopylae: The Battle that Changed the World* (2006).
[15] Something made very evident in the new book by George Cawkwell with the telling title *The Greek Wars: The Failure of Persia* (2006).
[16] All translations from Greek and Latin texts that appear in this essay are my own.

mouths be kept under guard, for people are freed, set loose to bark freedom now that dominion's yoke is snapped.' Aeschylus is nowhere near as single-minded or one-dimensional as many modern commentators and film makers, but the picture of the Persians as the arch-enemy of Greek freedom is clearly visible and was to be further developed by later writers.

In most of the famous Greek literature of Athens' heyday the same is evident: all non-Greeks were inferior and barbarians. But they were not all alike. Aristotle makes this clear (*Politics* 1327b.29-32), when he speaks of the Hellenic people situated between the raw and cold North/West of Europe, with spirited but unintelligent people, and the settled and warm Asia, with indolent but intelligent people. The Greeks thus had an intermediate character, managing to combine intelligence and temperament to constitute the Aristotelian golden mean of mankind and political ability: 'Hence it continues to be free and is the best-governed of all people, and if formed in one political union would be able to rule the world.' Aristotle is not alone in this assumption, in a short treatise ascribed to the great scholar and founder of scientific medicine, Hippocrates (but maybe not actually written by him), *On Airs, Waters, and Places,* the very same attitudes towards Greek and barbarian physiology is evident (chap. 16):

> With regard to the pusillanimity and cowardice of the inhabitants, the principal reason the Asiatics are more unwarlike and of gentler disposition than the Europeans is, the nature of the seasons, which do not undergo any great changes either to heat or cold, or the like; … It is changes of all kinds which arouse understanding of mankind, and do not allow them to get into a torpid condition. For these reasons, it appears to me, the Asiatic race is feeble, and further, owing to their laws; for monarchy prevails in the greater part of Asia.

Defining others as inferior and barbarians was significant in classical Greek thought and writing.[17] This way of thinking is of course connected to Greek thoughts about and attitudes towards slaves and slavery. Nearly all slaves were 'barbarians', and as long as the Greeks were superior and fit to rule, there was no reason to question the

---

[17] Cf. E. Hall, *Inventing the Barbarian: Greek Self-Definition through Tragedy* (Oxford: Clarendon Press, 1989), H.A. Khan (ed.), *The Birth of the European Identity: The Europe-Asia Contrast in Greek Thought 490-322 BCE* (1994), J.E. Coleman and C.A. Walz (eds.), *Greeks and Barbarians: Essays on the Interactions Between Greeks and Non-Greeks in Antiquity and the Consequences for Eurocentrism* (1997), T. Harrison (ed.), *Greeks and Barbarians* (Edinburgh: Edinburgh University Press, 2002) and B. Isaac, *The Invention of Racism in Classical Antiquity* (Princeton, N.J.: Princeton University Press, 2004), esp. pp. 255-298.

institution of slavery and all the more reason to acquire barbarian slaves. Slavery was common to many ancient societies, but few can be characterised as slave societies in the way that Athens was, relying heavily on slave labour in production.[18]

Athens came to lead the coalition of Greek city-states, known as the Delian League, formed in 477 BCE. The Delian League had started as a defence union against Persian aggression, but ended up as an Athenian empire. After decades of tension, minor battles and an unsuccessful attempt to liberate Egypt, a treaty was agreed with Persia in the mid-fifth century, known as the Peace of Callias. Persia continued to be the main enemy, but tension and strife among the major Greek cities increased, eventually leading to the clash between Athens and Sparta, the Peloponnesian War(s) in the years 431-403 BCE. The Persians were continuously called on by different parties and involved in Greek affairs during the whole of the fifth century, and Greek political leaders who were exiled or fled from domestic prosecution were more than happy to dwell in the Persian court. As the Spartans allied with them to defeat the Athenian fleet, the Persians once again got the upper hand along the Ionian coast. After more wars among the Greeks, Persia was the arbitrator in settling the peace and more or less able to dictate the new treaty in 386 BCE, known as the King's Peace. The treaty established Persian control over the Greek cities of Asia Minor and Persia remained the main foreign menace to Greece. And even though trade and mutual exchange with the Persians continued, so did derogatory speech and writing about them.

The picture of the peoples of the East as meek, decadent, untrustworthy and substandard beings was drawn in classical times in Greece. In particular it was sketched out by the Athenians as they also increasingly gained in self-confidence from their imperial successes. This first instance of 'orientalism' has been one of the long-lasting, but not so great legacies of classical Greece to the Western, European world. Yet, somewhat ironically, this legacy has been handed down to us thanks to the conquest *of* the Persian Empire by a semi-Greek monarch and pupil of Aristotle, Alexander the Great. Without the Hellenistic *koinê* culture that emerged in many of the lands he conquered in Anatolia and the Middle East, classical Greek literature would hardly have survived.

---

[18] On ancient slave societies see M. Finley, *Ancient Slavery and Modern Ideology* (New York, N.Y.: Penguin Books, 1983) and P. Cartledge, 'Rebels and Sambos in Classical Greece', in idem *Spartan Reflections* (London: Duckworth, 2001). On ancient views on superiority, imperialism and slavery, see B. Isaac, *The Invention of Racism in Classical Antiquity*, pp. 169-224.

Jon W. Iddeng

# Alexander the Great and the Hellenistic Period

After his father Philip had subdued the Greeks (338 BCE) and was murdered (336 BCE), the young Macedonian king Alexander fulfilled his mission to attack the Persian Empire in 334 BCE. Until the time of his death twelve years later he managed to conquer the whole Persian Empire, with its many provinces, peoples and cities who stood up against him, as well as peoples and land in the Far East that not even the Persian king had controlled. A pretext for the conquest was to revenge the Persian assault on Greek soil and to liberate the Greek city-states of the Anatolian coast from Persian rule. Alexander had learnt from his teacher, Aristotle, about Greek superiority, but also about the vast and rich lands in the East waiting to be explored and exploited. The campaign was clearly also an adventurous expedition and the entourage included many Greek scholars and scientists. It will never be clear whether or not Alexander started to believe in his own myth and divinity, but as his campaign went along from success to success, he clearly wanted to outdo heroes of the past such as Achilles and Heracles in the East and reach Dionysus's native soil.

Yet the Persian Empire was not converted into a Greek kingdom, rather Alexander became a Persian king. At least so it looked to many of his Greco-Macedonian companions, who started to criticise his habits of dressing in Persian style, his inclination for ritual greeting (*proskynesis*) and eastern luxury, and accordingly neglect of Macedonian court tradition. Ultimately this lead to discord, processes, executions, mutinies and the end of Alexander's imperial conquest, but also to the recruitment of easterners to Alexander's army and administration. Nursed on Greek propaganda, the Greco-Macedonian elite never saw the easterners and Persian elite as their equals. But did Alexander?

Much has been written about Alexander and his aim to fuse the races and create a brotherhood of mankind. Some of this literature has been based less on sound interpretation and source criticism than on a wishful reading of certain ancient claims about Alexander.[19] From Plutarch's *Life* and especially his *De Alexandri fortuna* we can learn about Alexander's philosophy that 'all things on earth should be subject to one logic and constitution and that all mankind should be one.' Arrian contributes to the story of Alexander's policy of fusion in his book 7, about the Susa wedding (7.4) and the famous prayer for common peace in Opis (7.11). Yet the mass wedding in Susa was predominantly a confirmation of relationships between Greco-Macedonian men and their local concubines, and the Opis prayer is for Persians and Macedonians to enjoy concord and community in governing the empire, not a blending of all

---

[19] E.g. J.G. Droysen, *Geschichte Alexanders des Grossen* (1833, 2nd ed. 1877), W.W. Tarn, *Alexander the Great* (1948) and R. Lane Fox, *Alexander the Great* (1973).

people within its border. Today few scholars share the past visions of a truly great Alexander, carrying the white man's burden of civilising and uniting people in a great commonwealth and 'brotherhood of mankind' as Tarn wrote 60 years ago.[20] Bosworth is more in line with today's *Stand der Forschung* when claiming:

> There was no attempt to intermix the Macedonian and Persian nobilities, if anything an attempt to keep them apart. In particular the Macedonians seem to have been cast as the ruling race... There is nothing here remotely resembling a deliberate policy to fuse together the two people into a single army. If there is any policy it is *divide et impera*.[21]

Alexander's conquest was nevertheless of great importance to our subject, as it brought Greece to the Middle East through his establishing Greek cities and administration on conquered soil, and it brought pieces of the Middle East to Greece as spoils and gifts.

This process continued as Alexander's generals and heirs, known as the *diadochi*, fought over and for Alexander's empire, and in the end headed dynasties of separate states. These kingdoms continued to collaborate and fight one another in the following Hellenistic period, as kingdoms have always done in the region. But as their leadership was of Greco-Macedonian origin they kept in contact with the Greek world, and craved for Greek goods and culture and thus kept up trading and distribution across vast distances. Alexander's conquest gave the Greek culture necessary *Lebensraum*, as has been claimed by later scholars. It started a process of Hellenising the Near East, but also of reinforcing Greek culture with a necessary foreign impetus. Alexandria, Antioch, Pergamum soon became new centres of cosmopolitan Greek culture and learning. Greek became the *lingua franca* in Anatolia and the Middle East. Eastern products, fashions and religious ideas were absorbed by the new urban upper-class and even brought to Greece. Yet it never truly became a mixed culture, as the Greeks settled in cities and were devoted to administration, trade and urban activities, and retained their own Greek customs and culture. The rustic parts of these Hellenistic states remained non-Greek, inhabited by local peasants and nomadic herdsmen. Locals had to adapt to Greek ways in order to make it in the urban centres and the state administration.[22]

---

[20] W.W. Tarn, *Alexander the Great* (1948; I), pp. 146-147.
[21] A.B. Bosworth, 'Alexander and the Iranians', *Journal of Hellenic Studies* 100 (1980), p. 20.
[22] Cf. the interesting study S. Averintsev, 'Ancient Greek "literature" and Near Eastern "writings": the opposition and encounter of two creative principles' (part 1 and 2), *Arion* 7.1 and 7.2 (2002).

# The Roman Empire

One by one these Hellenistic powers had to bow to Rome and Roman conquest from the second and early first century BCE. The Balkans, Anatolia, the Levant and finally Egypt were annexed and laid out as provinces of the Roman Empire. The eastern part of the Seleucid Empire broke away, though, and lost close contact with the Greek culture and the new West. From the old Persian mainland rose the Parthians, and even though they lost several battles with Rome, quite crucially under Trajan (98-117 CE), they always recovered and Mesopotamia never became Roman land. The Parthians therefore remained the major rival and arch enemy throughout Roman history, representing once again the deficient East.

In the East, Romans got to know a civilisation far older and more sophisticated than their own, and also riches and artefacts far beyond most people's imagination. Greek and Eastern people, art and treasures were brought to Rome, and with them Hellenistic traditions and cultures. Roman aristocrats started to fancy Eastern commodities, architecture and style. The Greek-Hellenistic culture and art had been copied for quite some time, but after Rome became master of the Eastern Mediterranean, Romans became acquainted with other Eastern products and customs as well. People started building in oriental style (even creating tombs in the shape of pyramids) and luxury products such as papyrus, silk, spices, incense and aromatics were imported into Rome by the ton. Pliny the Elder claims the deficit on trade with the east was 100 million sesterces a year ('This is what our extravagance and our women cost us') because the easterners did not buy any Roman products in return (*Natural History* 12.84). Many inhabitants of the empire were also involved in Eastern mysteries and cults.[23]

Although they started out as barbarians to the Greeks, Romans soon adopted Greek views about (and words for) foreigners, and included themselves in a Greco-Roman community of civilised people. To Romans the barbarians were by and large the people living outside the Roman borders and the *Pax Romana*, those not yet conquered and made into good citizens of the Roman Empire; and among these were the Parthians, although the many German tribes of the north were certainly the most feral. The non-Greek East, whether or not part of the Empire, was still met with

---

[23] On Hellenism, Hellenic culture and its influence on Romans, see E. Gruen, *The Hellenistic World and the Coming of Rome* (Berkeley, Calif.: University of California Press, 1984), idem *Studies in Greek Culture and Roman Politics* (Leiden: Brill, 1990), P. Green, *Alexander to Actium* (Berkeley, Calif.: University of California Press, 1990), and some relevant articles also in T. Fischer-Hansen (ed.), *East and West: Cultural Relations in the Ancient World* (Copenhagen: Museum Tusculanum Press, 1988). On Roman trade with the East, see G.K. Young, *Rome's Eastern Trade: International Commerce and Imperial Policy, 31 BCE-CE 305* (2001).

suspicion and prejudice.[24] Moreover, not all Romans entirely embraced Greeks and Hellenic culture either.

According to one myth Rome was settled by Trojan refugees, as outlined by the grand bard Vergil in *the Aeneid*, and many a Roman would know by heart his line 'I fear the gift-bringing Greeks'. In a sense Greeks were part of the depraved East. Stern moralists such as Cato the Censor deemed the Greeks as decadent and remained cool towards them. Such critics depicted the Greek way as soft and profligate, talkative and devious. Scipio was accordingly attacked for his Greek associates and preferences, and Marcus Antonius was denounced by the Augustan party for his interest not only in Cleopatra, but also in Eastern ways and *luxuria*. Augustus took great care to promote Roman values and religious tradition, also in opposition to 'foreign' Eastern ways and cults. Later emperors with too much fondness for Greek or Eastern culture and tradition, such as Nero, Domitian and Hadrian, received a bad press because of it. Magicians and astrologers, cynics and sophists, hypocrites and flatterers: all came from the Greek East, according to conservative Roman critics, and from time to time such groups were expelled from Rome en-bloc.[25] All in all, the Romans cherished and absorbed the Hellenistic culture of the East, but some were reluctant. Through their portrayal of the Greeks they kept alive the stereotype of the indulgent and aberrant East, which, by a twist of irony, they in turn had acquired from Greek literary tradition.

The Romans were quite tolerant towards foreign gods and religious practices; they even imported the fertility goddess Cybele from Phrygia in times of peril during the Second Punic War (even though they were anxious about her eunuch priests and only allowed public worship for one week each year). Yet, strange and foreign cults have a tendency to upset people, at least those who feel the status quo threatened by them. 'Who knows not what monsters demented Egypt worships?', the satirist Juvenal asks (*Satire* 15.1-2), after having condemned the Greeks and other Easterners in several of his satires, as dishonest flatterers and promiscuous wastrels. Religious conflicts shook the empire. Jewish resistance to the Roman imperial cult remained a great problem for Roman authorities for many years and led to two major revolts (66-70 and 132-135 CE) as well as anti-Semitism.[26]

When depicting the oriental East, conservative Romans also made sure to criticise its political organisation. Part of the stereotype of the bad East was autocracy

---

[24] Cf. H. Sonnabend, *Fremdenbild und Politik: Vorstellungen der Römer von Ägypten und dem Partherreich in der späten Republik und frühen Kaiserzeit* (1986).

[25] Cf. Segal (ed.), *Greece in Rome: Influence, Integration, Resistance*, Harvard Studies in Classical Philology, 97, (1998).

[26] B. Isaac, *The Invention of Racism in Classical Antiquity* (2004), pp. 440-491.

and despotism. In the classical Greek discourse this was a major part of anti-Persian propaganda, and thus something that also had to be turned against the Greek recent past. The tyrants were characteristic of sixth century Greece, and many had large popular support and introduced socio-political institutions typical to the later, proper polis society. The tyrants were belittled in the later Greek tradition, as were the early kings of Rome in later Roman tradition. Caesar's dictatorship and flirting with absolutism got him killed, and no emperor of the first 200 years could completely ignore the Roman people and senate, SPQR; and the term for king, *rex*, was completely avoided in the West. The political ideals of the Republic lived long in the senatorial elite into the Principate, and the idea was widespread that the Romans (as opposed to Eastern kingdoms) were governed not by an autocrat with absolute power, but by a constitutional monarch.[27] Emperors with high-handed conduct and divine aspirations, such as Domitian, ran into troublesome opposition and sometimes got assassinated. They were compared with Eastern despots. The Eastern rulers were also depicted by Romans as self-indulgent autocrats and their subjects as docile idolaters. Typical is Martial's claim (*Epigrams* 10.72), when addressing the new Emperor Trajan some time after the fall of Domitian, that the flattering pixies that had swayed him to sweet-talk the late emperor now should be off to eastern despots:

> In vain you come to me, Flatteries, you wretched creatures with shameless lips. I am not to speak of 'master and god'. There is no place for you now in this city. Off you go, ugly, abject beggars, far away to Parthians in turbans, to kiss the feet of tawdry kings. There is no master (*dominus*) here, but a commander-in-chief (*imperator*) and the most rightful of all senators.

Yet the Roman Emperor was a master, of course, with progressively greater powers also in the 'good' era of the Antonines. With Septimius Severus (193-211 CE), Rome got its first Emperor of Punic origin; his wife Julia Domna was of Syrian aristocracy, and later secured the throne for her grand-nephew of Eastern stock, Elagabalus. The third century CE, after the fall of the Severans, was a time of crisis, peril and war for the Roman Empire. The imperial frontiers were attacked in the north and east, and the commanders-in-chief in the years to follow had their hands busy fighting invading forces as well as each other, as different branches of the army hailed their own commanders as emperors. Quite a few of the emperors and usurpers in this period were 'barbarians', and some of those who made it in the official imperial

---

[27] Cf. S. Houby-Nielsen, 'Augustus and the Hellenistic kings: a note on Augustan propaganda', in T. Fischer-Hansen (ed.), *East and West: Cultural Relations in the Ancient World* (Copenhagen: Museum Tusculanum Press, 1988).

records were men from the East, such as Maximinus Thrax (235-238 CE) and Philip the Arab (244-249 CE).

By and large the Eastern part of the Empire became more and more important and gradually the centre was shifting eastwards. The elite of the Greek East had in the early imperial days remained attached to their own cities as was normal for the Greek city-states, but increasingly they became more involved in the central government and started to join the Roman aristocracy and Senate in numbers by the second century CE. Commodus' decree in 212 CE made all free inhabitants of the Empire Roman citizens, which spurred the Eastern citizens further to become involved in imperial government and administration. In the times of trouble the East had been shown to be more prosperous, urbanised and settled, easier to control and defended and more loyal to the Empire than parts of the West. And in the end, the administration of the Empire was divided and the emperor (or main emperor, when there was more than one) started to reside in the East, rather than in the West. Nicomedia, on the coast of the Sea of Marmara in Anatolia, was for a period the residential city of the Roman Emperor before Constantine redeveloped Byzantium into his new capital, Constantinople, and finalised the shift of weight from west to east.

## The Byzantine Period

A couple of generations later another phenomenon of Eastern origin had supplanted the traditional gods and hence the core of the Greco-Roman culture and mindset: Christianity. By Theodosius' edict of 391 CE, which prohibited academies, agonistic activities in the gymnasia and the arena and pagan worship, the Christianisation of the Empire may be seen as complete. It was not, however, any longer a complete and united empire. As northern tribes and people continued to invade and settle within what used to be the Western part of the Roman Empire, the Western provinces fell apart and the Western part of the empire ceased to exist. The unity of the Empire was not forgotten, but the various pieces proved hard to bring together under imperial rule, even for a wilful emperor as Justinian (527-65 CE). After 600 years the Eastern and Western parts of the Mediterranean were again separated, and the Western part disintegrated. The Eastern part of the empire, which we call the Byzantine Empire, remained the intellectual and political centre and the Emperor continued to rule the Balkans, Anatolia, the Levant and the shores and islands of the Eastern Mediterranean. The inhabitants still saw themselves as the true Romans, *Romanoi*, and continued as subjects to Constantinople. And they even still had to fight the Persians. The Sassanians had brought down the Parthian kings and ruled a new Persian Empire (224-651 CE) that caused the Romans a great deal of trouble. Valerian was defeated and captured by the Sassanians in 260, Diocletian fought hard battles with Narses (and won) at the end of the third century and Emperor Julian died in Mesopotamia during a campaign in 363 CE. The Byzantine Empire was at the brink of destruction, however, when the Persians under Chosroes II from 603 CE captured Anatolia, Syria, Palestine and Egypt (where churches were destroyed and Zoroastrianism instigated) and aimed at Constantinople. Heraclius, exarch of Carthage, seized power and managed by enormous will-power and mobilisation of all the sources of the Empire to drive the Persians back and regain most of the lost territory by 628. Both empires were exhausted after many large battles. When the Arab Muslims started their expansion a few years later, they took advantage of this fatigue to swiftly conquer the whole Arabian Peninsula, Persia and not long after northern Africa and Iberia. A large part of the Byzantine Empire and Christianity was subjugated, and France and Anatolia were endangered. A new Eastern arch-enemy had appeared, and a new volume in the book of East-West antagonism was to be written.

After Justinian there was no sufficient political desire or force to reunite the Roman Empire. The East and the West were united in Christianity, but the quarrels within the early Church lead to discord and schism. The Western Church was smaller and less significant in comparison with the multitude of congregations and parishes of the East. But the West had the pope, claming authority from Peter, and no strong emperor to overrule the Church. That proved to be an advantage, as the Pope and the Roman Catholic Church thus evolved as a major political force in the West; and, after the breach during the iconoclastic period (711-802 CE), increasingly in opposition to the Ecumenical Patriarch and the Orthodox Church in the East.[28] Hence a new chapter in the East/West controversy was opened; its subject was Christian doctrine and heresy. Later attempts to reunite the Church all failed, with the final schism coming in 1054, but a sense of Christian community was brought about in the wake of the Muslim conquests. To the good old Eastern stereotype was added a significant religious factor and the result was the birth of the Western picture of the demonic *Islamic* East.

Crusades to reconquer the lost Palestinian land and the Iberian Peninsula were launched in this spirit. Nonetheless, most of the Christian population of Syria, Palestine and other parts of the conquered territory were treated fairly by the Muslims and were quite indifferent to the shift in sovereignty and the relationship between the Byzantines and the Arabs were not all hostile.[29] The steam of the initial Arab conquest ran out and after the Shiite controversy there was an end also to a Muslim

---

[28] Cf. H. Chadwick, *East and West: The Making of a Rift in the Church from Apostolic Times until the Council of Florence* (Oxford: Oxford University Press, 2003).

[29] Cf. C.E. Bosworth, *The Arabs, Byzantium and Islam: Studies in Early Islamic History and Culture* (Aldershot: Ashgate, 1996).

world united under one caliph. Accordingly the Christian campaign of reconquest was at least partly a success. Yet the recapture of the Holy Land proved that the crusaders and the Byzantine Empire constituted no holy alliance. The Byzantine Empire was not prosperous enough to engage a large army and tried to make the crusaders fight their wars. Various gangs of crusaders, on the other hand, could be quite intolerable to the local inhabitants they encountered on their way, and once they got the taste of Constantinople's splendour they easily forgot about the holy mission. Eventually crusaders, different Christian naval powers of the Mediterranean and Byzantine forces caused each other more trouble than they did any Muslim enemy. In the end they were all driven off Palestinian soil and the Byzantine Empire was left with a broken back. Step by step, from the initial Battle of Manzikert in 1071 to the final capture of Constantinople in 1453, the remainder of the Roman Empire was absorbed by the new Muslim force in the region, the Turks.[30] The Ottoman Empire hence attained the role in European discourse as the Eastern menace and the Turks were bestowed with all the classical characteristics of the East.

## Epilogue

This short account has tried to show that the stereotype of the barbarians and an anti-Eastern discourse was developed in the literate culture of the Greeks in classical times, based on a genuine fear of the Persians, but also on an increasing smugness. The attitude towards the East was handed down to the Romans and occasionally exploited for political, private or satirical purposes by writers throughout antiquity, and thus prevailed for all those who could read. 'The light from the Acropolis' has never illuminated its Near Eastern neighbours, rather a nefarious shadow was cast on the East that has proved hard to dispose of.

---

[30] Cf. J. Riley-Smith (ed.), *The Oxford History of the Crusades* (Oxford: Oxford University Press, 2000) and J. Harris, *Byzantium and the Crusades* (London: Hambledon and London, 2003).

# The Genealogy of the 'Other': The Turks, Islam and Europe

## From the Renaissance to the Enlightenment

Mustafa Soykut

Islam appeared to Europe as a military threat as well as a cultural one in terms of representing the 'other', vis-à-vis Europe. Europe defined itself along the lines of Christendom, especially beginning with the conquests of Spain and Sicily by the Arabs in the eighth and the ninth centuries. As a result of the rapid Ottoman conquests in Eastern Europe, from the mid-fifteenth century onwards, when thinking of Islam, the European mind thought of the Ottoman Turks. While the image of Islam as well as that of the 'Turk' served to define 'Europeanness' as opposed to the 'other', this image gradually started to change towards the end of the seventeenth century with Ottoman decline.

The genealogy of image creation about Islam in Europe had three elements. The first was the military one; namely, the conquests undertaken by the Arabs in the Middle East, North Africa, Spain and Sicily between the seventh and the ninth centuries, in the lands that were considered to be the natural territories of Christendom. Due to these conquests, with the shrinking of Christendom to Europe there came the conquests of the Ottoman Turks in Eastern Europe, starting in the late fourteenth century. The second element was the theological problem arising with the arrival of Islam, the last religion of the Abrahamic Judeo-Christian line, which claimed to revise and replace Christianity as a universal religion. The third one was the general lack of political unity in Christendom (which was now Europe) that coincided with the peak of Muslim Arab and Ottoman expansion.

As to the theological issues, the relations between Christianity and Judaism have been problematic from the very beginning. It was the claim of Jesus to be the awaited Jewish Messiah that caused the rejection of the new religion by orthodox Jews. The relations between Christianity and Islam have been even more problematic, for it was the claim of Islam to perfect the divine revelation and to have replaced Christianity as the message of the last prophet, that caused the antagonism between the two religions.

On the other hand, the political structure of Medieval Europe was far from united. After the collapse of the Roman Empire, Europe had defined itself along the lines of *universitas Christiana*, in other words, that of Christendom, first against the barbarian pagans, and later against the Muslim Arabs. The *two-headedness* of the Holy Roman Empire, namely, the separation of the temporal and the religious authority in the figures of the Emperor and the Pope (who did not always agree with each other and were often in conflict), added to the political fragmentation of Christian Europe, excluding the territories of the Byzantine Empire in Eastern Europe politically from Western Christendom. In fact, it was the Byzantine Empire itself which had been often accused of heresy for not recognising the authority of the Roman Church, as well as for its so-called 'caesaro-papism', that is, the Byzantine emperors' interference in religious affairs, and the subjugation of the Patriarch of Constantinople almost to the status of a serf. In other words, while Western Christendom was ruled by a loose political congregation called the Holy Roman Empire and feudalism, the East, on the other hand, was characterised by a somewhat more unitary political structure.

There are a few important milestone events and dates in the image-creation process between the Islamic and the Western civilisations. The year 1071 marks the victory by the Seljuk Turks at the Battle of Manzikert (Malazgirt) against the Eastern Romans and their subsequent retreat and decline before the newly arising Muslim power. One year after this, in 1072, the city of Palermo in Sicily was reconquered by the Normans from the Arabs, Sicily having been an Arab Emirate for three hundred years. The second milestone is the year 1492 which marked the discovery of America by the Genoese Christopher Columbus under the auspices of Isabelle of Castille, and the same Queen's expulsion of the Spanish Jews following the fall of Granada in Andalusia, which was the last bastion of the Arab Muslim presence in the Iberian peninsula after eight hundred years of coexistence with the Christians. The second half of the fifteenth century marks not only the peak of the Renaissance in Italy and of the humanist movement, but also the fall of Constantinople in 1453 and that of Trebizond in 1461, the last house of Byzantine royalty in Asia Minor. Thus, in a sense, the Muslim power represented by the Arabs in Europe for eight hundred years passed into the hands of Ottoman Turks gradually, the transfer being concluded by the fall of Constantinople.

Some of the first examples of image creators about the Turks in Europe were precisely those Byzantine expatriates who fled from Anatolia and took refuge in Italy and especially in Venice. Theodoro Spandugino was one of these expatriates of Cantacuzene origin, whose great-grandfather had served the last Byzantine Emperor Constantine

Palaeologus. He wrote one of the first reliable histories of the Ottoman family and their state,[1] correctly tracing their origins back to the Oğuz tribe of the Turks, rather than the myth that the Turks were Scythians according to some, or Teucres, that is inhabitants of Troy, a popular myth believed by many Renaissance writers.

## The Council of Ferrara-Florence and the Humanist Popes

Another important figure pertinent to the crusader idea against the Ottomans was Cardinal Bessarion of Trebizond (c. 1400-1472). Bessarion came to Constantinople and became a clergyman, who was then elevated to receive the title Bishop of Nicaea (İznik). He went to the Council of Ferrara-Florence for the unification of the Eastern and the Western churches, where he was to represent the Byzantine clergy. The reason for the unification was political, namely to secure political and military aid against the expanding Ottoman armies from the Catholic world. On April 13th/14th, 1439 the *Oratio dogmatica pro unione* was read by Bessarion, which proclaimed the short-lived union of the Roman and the Byzantine Churches. However, the union never received ratification by the Synod in Constantinople.

Oddly enough, later on Bessarion embraced the Catholic faith and lost an election to become pope by eight votes to fifteen in 1455. One of the arguments that was used against his election was the fact that he still had a beard, even though he had converted to Catholicism, and insisted on wearing his Greek habit, which raised doubts about the sincerity of his conversion.[2] Bessarion had dedicated his life to two main aims, 'to organise a crusade to the end of saving Constantinople and Anatolia from the Turkish conquest; to defend as much as possible, the treasures of the Greek culture which fell into the hands of the infidels'.[3] Although his first wish never came true, he collected

---

[1] The most reliably annotated edition of the work is by Donald M. Nicol, *Theodore Spandounes: On the Origin of the Ottoman Emperors* (Cambridge: Cambridge University Press, 1997). Nicol's book is translated from the edition of C.N. Sathas, *Documents inédits relatifs à l'histoire de la Grèce au moyen âge*, IX (Paris, 1890), pp. 133-261: Theodoro Spandugnino, *Patritio Constantinopolitano, De la origine deli Imperatori Ottomani, ordini de la corte, forma del guerreggiare loro, rito, et costumi de la natione*. Another smaller undated version in manuscript form is in Biblioteca Apostolica Vaticana: Theodoro Spandugino, *Relatione di Theodoro Spandugino patritio costantinopolitano. Ordine de la origine de principi de Turchi et della corte e costumi loro et della natione* (Città del Vaticano: Biblioteca Apostolica Vaticana: Barb. Lat. 5342).

[2] Kenneth M. Setton, *The Papacy and the Levant (1204-1571)*, vol. II (Philadelphia: The American Philosophical Society, 1978), p.162: Marino Zorzi, 'Cenni sulla vita e sulla figura di Bessarione', in Gianfranco Fiaccadori (ed.), *Bessarione e l'Umanesimo* (Napoli: Vivarium, 1994), p. 2.

[3] Gaetano Platania, 'L'Europa orientale e l'unione delle chiese', in Gianfranco Fiaccadori (ed.), *Bessarione e l'Umanesimo* (Napoli: Vivarium, 1994), p. 249. This and all other translations from Italian texts in this essay are my own.

and bought a large number of Greek manuscripts, which ended up in the Biblioteca Marciana of Venice, making a great contribution to humanist studies and the revival of the learning of ancient Greek language and culture in Renaissance Italy.[4]

Perhaps Bessarion's most important work was his letter in the nature of an invitation to war against the Turks, which he wrote to another clergyman of the same name, Bessarion the monk, upon the occasion of the conquest of Negroponte (Euboea) in Greece by the Turks in 1470.[5] In his letter he proposed a strategy that became a model for the following two centuries for those who called for crusades against the Turks. Between then and 1683 there came a whole lineage of political strategists, most of whom were high-ranking men of the papacy, starting with Bessarion in the 1470s and followed by Lazzaro Soranzo in 1598,[6] Marcello Marchesi[7] soon after, Angelo Petricca da Sonnino[8] in 1640 and Friar Paul de Lagny[9] in 1679, on the eve of the second siege of Vienna. Bessarion wrote in 1470: 'Let us not wait until the Turk attacks Italy. Believe me that he looks and aspires to this, and is mobilising and working to this end, with all [his] forces and industry. I will say it, and I will say it explicitly "O God, what grief", if he fulfils his dream.'[10] This strategy consisted of the necessity

---

[4] According to an inventory in 1473, his books number 1024 in the Venetian library. Marino Zorzi, 'Cenni sulla vita e sulla figura di Bessarione', in Gianfranco Fiaccadori (ed.), *Bessarione e l'Umanesimo* (Napoli: Vivarium, 1994), p 8.

[5] The copy of his letter to the monk Bessarion that the present author studied is included in the book of Scipione Ammirato, *Orazioni del Signor Scipione Ammirato a diversi principi intorno ai preparimenti che s'avrebbono a farsi contra la potenza del Turco. Aggiuntioni nel fine le lettere & orazioni di Monsignor Bessarione Cardinal Niceno scritte a Principi d'Italia* (Fiorenza: Per Filippo Giunti, 1598), (Biblioteca Apostolica Vaticana: Ferraioli. IV. 1794). It must be presumed that there are various copies of the letters that he wrote to Bessarion the monk and the orations dedicated to the rulers of Italy to promote a crusade against the Turks. They were written originally either in Latin or in Greek, since there are minor variations in the Italian text, which might indicate a translation into Italian from another language.

[6] Lazaro Soranzo, *L'Othomanno*, Vittorio Baldini-Stampatore Camerale (Ferrara: Vittorio Baldini, Stampatore Camerale, 1598).

[7] Monsignor Marcello Marchesi, *Five Treatises on 'The war against the Turk'*, (17th century): *1) Alla Santità di nostro Signore Papa Paolo Quinto Beatissimo Padre, 2) Alla Maestà del Re Catholico Filippo III. Sacra Catholica Maestà, 3) All'Illustrissimo et Eccellentissimo Signore Duca di Lerma, 4) Alla Maestà del Re d'Ungheria Mathia II. Sacra Maestà, 5) Del detto quinto trattato proemio, divisione, et ordine* (Città del Vaticano: Biblioteca Apostolica Vaticana: Barb. Lat. 5366.)

[8] Angelo Petricca Da Sonnino, *Trattato del modo facile d'espugnare il Turco, e discacciarlo dalli molti Regni che possiede in Europa. Composto dal padre Maestro Angelo Petricca da Sonnino Min: Conven: già Vicario Patriarcale di Constantinopoli, Commissario gn`le in Oriente, e Prefetto de Missionarij di Valacchia, et Moldavia. Dedicated to Cardinal Antonio Barberino. 10 Maggio 1640* (Città del Vaticano: Biblioteca Apostolica Vaticana: Barb. lat. 5151.)

[9] Da Lagni, Fra Paolo, *Memoriale di frà Paolo da Lagni cappuccino al pontefice Innocenzo XI nel quale si dimostra la necessità de' Principi Cristiani di prevenire il Turco col dichiarargli la guerra, 1679* (Città del Vaticano: Biblioteca Apostolica Vaticana: Vat. lat. 6926).

[10] Scipione Ammirato, op. cit., p. 3.

of attacking the Ottomans with an all-Christian, or at least all-Italian alliance, without waiting for them to attack first, in order to defeat the Ottomans once and for all. The justification for such a strategy was the belief that whenever the Ottomans attacked first, they won. In other words, the proposal was to convert the military confrontation with the Turks from a defensive into an offensive war, a strategy that was to be proposed again and again later by those mentioned above. However, Bessarion himself was conscious of the fact that the disunity among the Italian rulers was what prevented them from launching a decisive attack: 'Some say "What do we have to do with the Greeks or the Bulgarians or with the Dalmatians, or with the Hungarians. Let them go to hell, what is it to us? We are fine, let the others lose… It is the job of the Venetians. It serves them right. It would be better, if they suffered more harm."'[11]

Bessarion is one of the first men of the Renaissance, in a long and established tradition of Italian humanists within the political literature, to identify the ancient Greeks and the Romans with the Renaissance idea of 'civilisation' and Christendom, and to identify the Turks with the enemies of the ancient Greeks, that is, with the Persians. The use of antiquity as a legitimising factor, which so often served to apply concepts of the past to situations from the present, which was a characteristic of the Renaissance civilisation, was also used by Bessarion in his aforementioned work. He is speaking through the mouth of the Athenian orator Demosthenes (fourth century BC), placing the Turks in the position of Philip II of Macedonia, the Italians in the position of the Athenians, and himself as Demosthenes.[12] In his bellicose oration Bessarion warns the Italians in the following way:

> Certainly great and without comparison is his power. His [the Turk's] appetite cannot be sated, infinite is his greed for domination, and together with the science of war, he finds himself in the blossom of his age, having a trained body, strengthened in the hardships of war… Do you think that he has incurred such great expense and put soldiers in so many dangers, and in so many contrasting seasons engaged in most important undertakings, to dominate the small state of the Bulgarians, or the arid mountains of the Serbs, or the poverty of the Dalmatians? For the riches of Italy, I say, for the fertility of the country, for the sweetness of the fruits and for this light itself, in which he desires to live.[13]

---

[11] Scipione Ammirato, op. cit., pp. 4-5.
[12] *Persuasione del Reverendissimo Bessarione, Cardinale Niceno, agli Illustrissimi et Incliti Principi d'Italia. Dalla autorità di Demostene* in Scipione Ammirato, op. cit.
[13] Scipione Ammirato, op. cit., p.18

Two years after the fall of Euboea a crusade was planned under Pope Sixtus IV in 1472. This was the first action that he undertook after becoming pope a year before, and Bessarion was sent to France as the legate to convince the king of an anti-Turkish crusade. The whole campaign was a fiasco and it 'achieved little beyond the bringing back to Rome of twenty-five Turkish prisoners, who were paraded in triumph through the streets of the city.'[14]

The following years mark the incursion of Ottoman raider armies into the territories of the Venetian Republic in the north-eastern region of Italy known as Friuli. From 1468 onwards, the Ottoman armies started attacking the north-eastern territories of Italy, culminating in the 1478 incursion where the Ottoman armies reached the river Isonzo (which runs very close to the city of Venice) and terrified the people as well as the Venetian government. The following year the Venetians yielded. The 1479 peace treaty was signed between the Venetians and the Ottomans, the Venetians having to pay some 10,000 *ducati* to the Ottomans as well as handing over the islands of Scutari, Croia, Negroponte, Lemnos and Maina in the Eastern Mediterranean. This had an effect on political relations between the Italian states, as Venice embarked upon new conquests on the mainland of Italy, having lost its substantial number of trading colonies in the Eastern Mediterranean to the Ottomans.

Another important milestone in the creation of the Turkish image was the fall of the city of Otranto to the Ottomans in the following year of 1480. The city which was, like the rest of southern Italy, Aragonese territory, witnessed according to contemporary sources the slaughter of some 800 soldiers and civilians on the Minerva hill near the city, which is still remembered and commemorated in Otranto today as a symbol of martyrdom in the face of the infidel Turks.[15]

It is important to note that the image the Turk enjoyed in Italy throughout the Renaissance as well as in the following sixteenth and seventeenth centuries differed in Venice from anywhere else in Italy. Venice was the major political and commercial partner of the Ottomans, as opposed to Rome, which was the head of Catholic Christendom and had been the head of European Christendom until the Reformation. While most of the time Venice preferred to maintain peaceful coexistence with the Ottomans, being careful not to irritate them, the Roman Church preferred the crusader rhetoric at every possible opportunity. Understandably enough, such a state of continual

---

[14] 'Pope Sixtus IV', *The Catholic Encyclopaedia*, [www.newadvent.org/cathen/14032b.htm.]

[15] Cosimo Damiano Fonseca (ed.), *Otranto 1480. Atti del convegno internazionale di studio promosso in occasione del V. centenario della caduta di Otranto ad opera dei Turchi. (Otranto, 19-23 maggio 1980)*, Volumes 1 and 2 (Lecce: Galatina Congedo Editore, 1986).

war was detrimental to the commercial life of Venice. Hence Venice found itself most of the time opposing the Papacy in favour of the Ottomans in a spirit of *realpolitik*.[16]

One of the most important popes of his age in his anti-Turkish crusade plans was Pope Pius II (19th August 1458-15th August 1464), a contemporary of Cardinal Bessarion. He is also the author of the famous *Epistula ad Mahumetem* ('Letter to Muhammad'), inviting Mehmet II, conqueror of the second Rome, to convert to Christianity and to rule the world together with the ruler of the original Rome, named *Kızıl Elma* ('Red Apple') by the Byzantines and the Ottomans alike. This is a myth of the Byzantine as well as of the Ottoman imagination.[17] Pius' letter was never sent to Mehmet, however, it remained a classic of fifteenth-century political rhetoric. Nonetheless, many other works of Pius II reached large audiences of his time as well as posterity such as *La Discritione de l'Asia et Europa,* composed sometime between the fall of Constantinople in 1453 and the fall of Trebizond in 1461. In his work Pius says the following about the Turks:

> Of the origin, descent, life, dress and customs of the Turks
>
> I warn many of our age, not writers or poets but rather historians who are still involved with the error of thinking the Turks to be the Teucres. I believe, therefore, that they presume [this], for the Turks possess Troy, which was the habitation of the Teucres, however, those [Teucres] traced their origin back to Crete and Italy. The Turkish people are Scythic[18] and barbarian: whose origin and progress (although it [their progress] seems out of every proportion) I presume not to be completely alien, now that in our times these people have conquered with such a vigour that, dominating Asia and Greece, they have dispersed the Latins and the Christians. This narration will further shed light on the affairs of Thrace, from where our reasoning commenced. The Turks, as the philosopher Ethico says, had their fatherland beyond the Pyrenean Mountains [sic!] on the Nordic Ocean. They are cruel and ignoble people, and being ardent in every manner of luxury, they eat those things that others would abhor, such as the meat of wild animals,

---

[16] Giovanni Pillinini, 'Un discorso inedito di Paolo Paruta', in *Archivio Veneto,* ser V, LXXIV (Venezia: 1964).

[17] Ettore Rossi, 'La leggenda turco-bizantina del Pomo Rosso', in *Studii Bizantini e Neoellenici,* vol. V, 1937.

[18] The word scytico ('scitico' in contemporary spelling) or Scyta (scita) apart from denoting the ancient people of Asia, the Scythians (of Iranian stock), was also synonymous with 'barbarian'. See G. Alessio and C. Battisti, *Dizionario Etimologico Italiano,* Vol. V (Firenze: Barbèra Editore, 1975), pp. 3403-4.

wolves and vultures, and neither would they abstain from the excretions of the immature parts of the body.[19]

A much more favourable view of the Turks was put forward by the famous Venetian historiographer Francesco Sansovino who depicted a more enlightened vision of the Ottoman princes within the Renaissance framework, drawing similarities between the figures of Greco-Roman antiquity and certain Ottoman sultans. Mehmet the Conqueror was one of the most controversial figures in the historiography about the Ottomans as well as a legend in his own lifetime. He was the one who invited the Italian Renaissance artist Gentile Bellini from Venice to produce his famous portrait. Oddly enough, Mehmet the Conqueror portrayed himself as a European ruler, using the title *kayser-i diyār-ı Rūm* ('Caesar of the Roman Lands') for the first and the last time among the Ottoman sultans.

In the book entitled, *Gli Annali Turcheschi overo Vite de' Principi della Casa Othomana* [The Turkish Annals, and the lives of the princes of the House of Osman] published in Venice in 1573 Francesco Sansovino writes about Mehmet II and his successors as follows:

> [Mehmet was] very shrewd and had a bright intelligence, because of which he was interested in various things. Besides other things, he was very fond of the study of astrology and used to say that he had foreseen, thanks to that science, that he would become the ruler of the world. Apart from this, he knew five languages besides his natural one, since he certainly spoke Greek, Latin, Arabic, Chaldean[20] and Persian. He took extreme pleasure in reading great things in these languages, above all the matters on Caesar and Alexander the Great, whom he had sought to imitate, enjoying very much being considered another Alexander the Great.[21]

---

[19] Pio II. (Enea Silvio Piccolomini), *La Discritione de l'Asia et Europa di Papa Pio II* (Vinegia: Appresso Vicenzo Vaugris a 'l segno d'Erasimo, 1544), pp. 187 V-188 R. The *Discritione de l'Asia et Europa di Papa Pio II,* which was published in Venice in 1544, is most probably the unfinished work of Pius II on *the description of the world known in his times,* See R. Aubenas and R. Ricard, *Storia della chiesa dalle origini fino ai giorni nostri. XV La Chiesa e il Rinascimento* (Torino: Editrice S. A. I. E., 1963), p. 69. It must have been written sometime between 1453 and 1461. In his book there is the narrative of the conquest of Constantinople, but one understands that Trebizond had not yet fallen (1461).
[20] Also called Chaldaic, it is synonymous with the biblical language Aramaic, called also Syriac.
[21] Francesco Sansovino, *Gli Annali Turcheschi overo Vite de' Principi della Casa Othomana* (Venetia: 1573), p. 151.

> [Bayezid II] enjoyed peace, as he had a serene soul and a pleasurable nature. He was intelligent and used to study philosophy and especially he liked the works of Averroës.[22] He was in brief, a prince of good nature.[23]

> [Selim I] was especially fond of the leaders of antiquity like Alexander the Great and Caesar the Dictator, and he was always reading their affairs translated into the Turkish language.[24]

He also makes the following positive remark in the introduction to his book:

> I have always maintained… that the greatness and power of the Turkish nation deserves much consideration. As a result of seeing their ancient military institution and the order of their civil government, one must conclude, as it is evident, that they are men of valour, and not at all rough. As to the military, I do not see any other people among ours that has better order, or is more reminiscent of the Roman order, than the Turkish one. Considering that they, almost as successors of the aforementioned Romans, are abstinent in war, resistant to fatigue and obedient to their superiors…[25]

However, such praise of the barbaric Turks was the exception rather than the rule as far as public opinion was concerned. Most of the time the comparisons made between antiquity and the Turks were negative ones. The reason is that the Turks represented the Persians and the barbarians, and Christendom represented civilisation itself. This was engraved on the collective memory of the rulers and of the intellectuals of the time, and was later transformed by the Renaissance culture into archetypes of the 'civilised world' as opposed to the 'barbarians': the civilised world as represented by Athens and Greece, the barbarians as represented by the Persians, transformed now into Italy as opposed to the barbarian Turks.[26]

---

[22] i.e. Ibn Rushd. 1126 Cordoba-1198 Marrakesh.
[23] Francesco Sansovino, op. cit., p. 171.
[24] Francesco Sansovino, op. cit., p. 204.
[25] Francesco Sansovino, op. cit., foreword.
[26] Francesco Tateo, 'L'Ideologia umanistica e il simbolo "immane" di Otranto', in Cosimo Damiano Fonseca (ed.), *Otranto 1480. Atti del convegno internazionale di studio promosso in occasione del V. centenario della caduta di Otranto ad opera dei Turchi. (Otranto, 19-23 maggio 1980)*, Volume 2, (Lecce: Galatina Congedo Editore, 1986.)

Mustafa Soykut

# The Sixteenth Century and the 'Invincible' Turk

The naval defeat at Lepanto (Náupaktos) in 1571 is one of the milestones (together with the fall of Constantinople and the second siege of Vienna) that affected the image of the Turk in Europe. The Battle of Lepanto changed the image of the invincible Turk in Europe. The crusader alliance under Don John of Austria, with the participation of Venice, Spain and Genoa, defeated the Ottoman fleet and put an end to Ottoman naval supremacy in the Eastern Mediterranean. However, the Ottoman fleet revived after a short time and the land forces were unaffected. An example of the short-lived post-Lepanto euphoria that spread throughout the whole of Europe following the Ottoman naval defeat is characterised by the following Venetian sonnet of the time:

> Well, Signor Selim, it has been of velvet the league of our baptised ones [Christians]: sixty thousand Turks and the converted, with three hundred sails of yours went into the broth.
>
> Charon[27] awaits their souls at the swamp: Ali, Piale, with the other sons of Allah. Let your Mohammed (?) now, with those *paşas* of yours, medicate the defeat you have had.
>
> What did you think, that you could have fooled Italy and Spain with your rascals? Did you think that Muhammad could beat Christ?
>
> Rome [Pius V], the Eagle [Spain], and the Lion with paws [Venice] can easily pass the straits [the Dardanelles], thus behold and hear their cannons, arquebuses and their swords.[28]

Ironically enough, Uluç Ali Reis, known as Occhialì in Italy, was a Calabrian *rinnegato* (i.e. convert) who showed great resistance to the Genoese fleet at Lepanto. His battalion was the only one to remain intact of the Ottoman fleet![29]

In the following decades, as well as during the sixteenth century in general, the popularity of books on the Turks in Italy was so great that one of the advocates of

---

[27] The ferryman of Greek mythology who carries the condemned souls on a ship through the Hell's swamp Styx.
[28] (Anonymous, Miscellanea Marciana, 169,2), in Guido Antonio Quarti, *La Battaglia di Lepanto nei Canti Popolari Dell'Epoca* (Milano: Istituto Editoriale Avio-Navale, 1930), pp. 128-129.
[29] Lucetta Scaraffia, *Rinnegati. Per una Storia dell'Identità Occidentale* (Roma-Bari: Laterza, 1993), p. viii.

the crusade, Lazzaro Soranzo published his book on espionage called *Othomanno*[30] in 1598, during the war in Hungary. Although Soranzo was a Venetian, the Venetian Senate did not permit the book to be published in Venice as it was a time of peace with the Ottomans. Therefore it was published in Ferrara instead, which was papal territory. At the end of the book he writes:

> However, I knew from experience that it was impossible if not uncomfortable to get hold of them, since there were many of them disseminated across various countries, and, furthermore, that indecent and afflicted people were eagerly starting to publish books that took the Turks as a subject. Publishing houses will publish books of little value on any subject (for which this century is to be blamed) as long as people are curious to read about it; and now they are curious to read about the Turks.[31]

The following (seventeenth) century was an important one for the crusader idea of mobilising Europe under the auspices of the papacy. Among peoples of non-European origin, the Ottoman Turks who entered on the European scene towards the end of the fourteenth century left an indelible mark on the cultural, political and military life of Europe, which was to last until the beginning of the twentieth century, when it suffered the same fate as its centuries-old rival the Habsburg Empire. It ended in 1923 with the proclamation of the new Turkish Republic. Europe, which identified itself in terms of Christendom and the *Pax Romana* until the Renaissance, saw all of these peoples of 'foreign' descent as the threat *par excellence* to *Christianitas*. According to Kenneth Setton, the special position the Ottomans had was due to the fact that: 'From the later fourteenth century to the beginning of the twentieth, Europeans tended to identify Islam with the Ottoman Empire.'[32] The official head of Christianity, at least until the Reformation, the papacy made several attempts at eradicating these foreign presences from Europe. This was institutionalised by a series of holy wars which we call the crusades.

---

[30] Lazzaro Soranzo, *L'Othomanno*, Vittorio Baldini-Stampatore Camerale (Ferrara: Vittorio Baldini, Stampatore Camerale, 1598).
[31] Lazzaro Soranzo, op.cit., extract from the last words of the book.
[32] Kenneth M. Setton, *Western Hostility to Islam and Prophecies of Turkish Doom* (n.p., American Philosophical Society, 1992), p.17.

Mustafa Soykut

# Towards the Thirty Years War and Beyond

These later crusader ideas of the seventeenth century organised by the Holy See against the Ottomans, during the Thirty Years War and after the Westphalian settlement, the projects or rather exhortations to wage war against the Turks can be illustrated here by the testimony of two unpublished Vatican manuscripts. Their authors are two prominent yet little known members of the Holy See, Monsignor Marcello Marchesi and Angelo Petricca da Sonnino. The importance of these men, together with a later manuscript by a certain Friar Paolo da Lagni (Paul de Lagny, originally a French Capuchin friar) presented to Pope Innocent XI in 1679,[33] lies in the fact that, starting with Marchesi, they are the papal authors of a series of seventeenth century 'bellicose exhortations' that inspired the Holy See to undertake (and not only to undertake but also to finance as in the case of Poland)[34] a defence of Christendom against the Turks, culminating in the defence of Vienna in 1683.

The first manuscript from the Vatican library, belongs to Marcello Marchesi's first letter in his bellicose exhortation to Pope Paul V (16th May 1605-28th January 1621).[35] There is a dearth of information about Marchesi given his importance, for he was one of the main papal architects of the seventeenth-century crusader plans against the Ottomans. C. Eubel, in his *Hierarchia Catholica Medii et Recentioris Aevi*, writes that Marchesi was born in Varzi, a province of the northern Italian city of Pavia. He was the bishop of Senj in Croatia and held the office of 'scribe of the archive of Curia Romana'. He was sacerdotal doctor in *utroque jure* (in both civil and canonical

---

[33] Fra Paolo Da Lagni, *Memoriale di frà Paolo da Lagni cappuccino al pontefice Innocenzo XI nel quale si dimostra la necessità de' Principi Cristiani di prevenire il Turco col dichiarargli la guerra, 1679* (Città del Vaticano: Biblioteca Apostolica Vaticana: Vat. lat. 6926).

[34] See Gaetano Platania, *Venimus, Vidimus et Deus vicit. Dai Sobieski ai Wettin. La diplomazia pontifica nella Polonia di fine seicento* (Cosenza: Edizioni Periferia, 1992.); Platania, 'Innocent XI Odescalchi et l'esprit de "croisade"' in *XVIIe Siècle. La Reconquête Catolique en Europe Centrale* (n.p., Société d'Étude du XVIIe Siècle, Avril-Juin 1998.); Platania, 'Diplomazia e guerra turca nel XVII secolo. La politica diplomatica polacca e la "lunga guerra turca" (1673-1683)', in Giovanna Motta (ed.), *I Turchi, il Mediterraneo e l'Europa* (Milano: Franco Angeli s.r.l., 1998.); Platania, 'Santa Sede e sussidi per la guerra contro il turco nella seconda metà del XVII secolo', in *Il Buon Senso o la Ragione. L'Università degli Studi della Tuscia* (Viterbo: Sette Città, 1997).

[35] Monsignor Marcello Marchesi, *Five Treatises on 'The war against the Turk* (17th century): *1) Alla Santità di nostro Signore Papa Paolo Quinto Beatissimo Padre, 2) Alla Maestà del Re Catholico Filippo III. Sacra Catholica Maestà, 3) All'Illustrissimo et Eccellentissimo Signore Duca di Lerma, 4) Alla Maestà del Re d'Ungheria Mathia II. Sacra Maestà, 5) Del detto quinto trattato proemio, divisione, et ordine* (Città del Vaticano: Biblioteca Apostolica Vaticana: Barb. Lat. 5366).

law) and the 'prothonotary apostolic'[36] (a member of the highest college of prelates in the Roman Curia) and apostolic secretary, and died on 1st August 1613.[37] As can be concluded from the second letter in the manuscript written by Marchesi to King Philip III of Spain, he was present at the battles of Keresztes (*Kerestis*) in 1596 and of Kanizsa (*Canisia*) in Hungary in 1601. In his letter to Pope Paul V, Marchesi provides many details about these battles, and makes some very interesting comments on the military failure of the European states against the Ottomans, claiming that the Christian states had been incapable of producing alternative methods of fighting the Turks, in the face of the Ottoman armies' profoundly different military strategies.

> It is this therefore that is the particular and the very cause why we have ordinarily lost and in the end are still losing against the Turks, because we do not know the art of fighting such enemies; they abound in cavalry (light cavalry for the most part) and fight encircling mostly from a distance without order and in an unpredictable manner, furtively and from the back without letting themselves be attacked or reached; a different way from the Roman one and from the one used among us, and not knowing how to beat them, we are either defeated at battle or in any way they remain the masters of the expedition.[38]

Marchesi's aim in his letter to Pope Paul V (16th May 1605-28th January 1621) was to promote a general war of Christians against the Ottomans. His manuscript to the Pope is the work of an experienced military strategist as well as a top ranking clergyman of the Holy See. The manuscript's date is unknown, however considering the aforementioned dates, it must have been composed between 1606 and 1613, not many years later than 1606, after the peace signed between the Austrians and the

---

[36] Prothonotary apostolic is 'a member of the highest college of prelates in the Roman Curia, and also of the honorary prelates on whom the Pope has conferred this title and its special privileges. In later antiquity there were in Rome seven regional notaries, who, on the further development of the papal administration and the accompanying increase of the notaries, remained the supreme palace notaries of the papal chancery (*notarii apostolici* or *protonotarii*). In the Middle Ages, the prothonotaries were very high papal officials, and were often raised directly from this office to the cardinalate. Sixtus V (1585-90) increased their number to twelve. Their importance gradually diminished, and at the time of the French Revolution the office had almost entirely disappeared. On 8 February, 1838, Gregory XVI re-established the college of real prothonotaries with seven members called "protonotarii de numero participantium", because they shared in the revenues.' *The Catholic Encyclopaedia*, 'Prothonotary apostolic' [http://www.newadvent.org/cathen/12503a.htm].
[37] C. Eubel (ed.), *Hierarchia Catholica Medii et Recentioris Aevi*, vol. IV (Regensburg: Sumptibus et Typis Librariae Regensbergianae Monasterii: 1935), p.309.
[38] Marcello Marchesi, op. cit., 10 V.

Ottomans after the long war in Hungary (the Peace of Zidvatoruk), and obviously before his death in 1613. Not only does the manuscript provide the reader with an image of the Turks as perceived in military, cultural and religious matters, but it also gives a Christendom's view of itself seen through the eyes of the Catholic world. Marchesi starts his letter to Pope Paul V as follows:

> It is beyond doubt that the resolutions and efforts realised by Christian princes on land and on sea against the Turks at different times, have been astonishing, however, not less astonishing has been the infelicity of the events, having the Turks in the end always gain superiority, and acquire in such a short time such a great empire. Of whose prosperity and our infelicity, various reasons have been put forward.[39]

Marchesi is totally dissatisfied with the European nobility, almost in a contemptuous manner. According to him, the nobility is lost in the pleasures of court life, paying no attention to the real concerns such as the military. Furthermore, he thinks 'no army has much discipline (if any at all) and has little modesty, sobriety and obedience, and little tolerance of fatigue and discomfort, as well as, little hope of rewards, as can be seen.'[40] Compared to Angelo Petricca da Sonnino, the author of the second manuscript, Marchesi emphasises much more the cultural and religious aspects of the failure against the Turks. Although both Marchesi and da Sonnino represent the point of view of the Catholic Church, da Sonnino's manuscript should be read in the context of military and political rhetoric on the 'Turkish question'. Although Marchesi is also utterly concerned with the military aspects, as he himself was on the battlefield in the war of Hungary, the letter written to Paul V presents the reader with a self-portrait of Christendom as perceived by a leading member of the Catholic Church of the early seventeenth century, where religion alone was no longer the only factor to determine the politics of the day, in a period when the importance of the papacy was in decline as a result of religious fragmentation in Europe. It is precisely in this period that the Catholic Church seized the opportunity of the old rhetoric of the crusade or 'just war' against the infidel Turks, in a way to direct attention away from the religious fragmentation that was still taking place on the eve of the Thirty Years War.

Marchesi begins by refuting the point of view that Christianity as a religion is responsible for the lack of success in combating the Turks. His polemic about Luther's position, quoted below, reflects not only the acceptance by the Catholic Church of the

---

[39] Marcello Marchesi, op. cit., 1 R.
[40] Marcello Marchesi, op. cit., 2 V.

legitimacy of a 'just war' against the Turks, but also reflects the Catholic antipathy towards the Protestants within the spirit of the Counter-Reformation. In fact, from the very beginning of the confrontation with the newly arising universal-religion of Islam, as well as with the Reformation question, the fight against the 'infidels' and the 'heretics', was not only considered equally legitimate from a theological point of view, but it also was institutionalised under the concept of 'just war'. Marchesi writes:

> First of all, some heretics have denied the Christians the legitimacy of waging war, not to mention war against the Turks. Furthermore, Luther madly preached by saying, not only not to wage war against the Turks, but even not to show resistance in order not to oppose the Divine Will, for God through them castigates us. So do other heretics, or rather atheists claim, as the nobles have already claimed, the Christian religion to be a threat to the Republic and the mundane state, having put an end to the gallantry of antiquity [as a result of] having ruined the Roman Empire.[41]

In his dispute against Luther, he further says:

> and that faceless Luther had to be ashamed, as later he was, of having let himself indulge too much in hatred of the Pope, that he desired to see the whole of Christianity go as soon as possible under the Turk, so as to be able to see the extinction of the name of the Pope. Preaching, therefore, not to resist the Turk, in order not to oppose divine castigation, as if we did not have to find remedies in the case of plague, famine and other public castigation...[42]

What is referred to here is Luther's initial proposition that waging war against the Turks was a sin, as it would have been opposing the divine will, for Luther thought that the Turks were the divine punishment of God for the sins committed by Christendom. Luther modified his proposition after the first siege of Vienna by Süleyman the Magnificent in 1529 and invited the German princes to fight the Turks.

The aristocrats are also pictured as licentious and indulgent people by Marchesi. As a result, their negligence of military matters results in Europe being plagued by the Turks. The author also views the jurists and the intellectuals with equal contempt, seeing them as an obstacle in gaining victory over the Turks. For they are also responsible for engaging excessively in intellectual debates, which are nothing

---

[41] Marcello Marchesi, op. cit., 1 V.
[42] Marcello Marchesi, op. cit., 6 R.

but a waste of time and intellectual vanity. He thinks that 'jurisprudence has grown into too many constitutions and commentaries, and into too many tricks against the intention of our Legislator Christ: who handed down morals and ceremonials, but no judgements.'[43] As he praises the codification of the thereto existing laws by Emperor Justinian (527-565), and shows an antipathy towards the intellectuals, one almost senses a craving for authoritarianism in Marchesi:

> Among the Christians the majority of the people occupy their time with vain things, games, pastimes and various handicrafts, a great deal of which are unnecessary and unreasonable both in public and in private, spending in them their time and their fortunes as in unnecessary devices... Moreover, among the Christians people get occupied with useless, or even harmful sciences and letters, among other things with the legal and judicial profession ... [These very people] attract the infinite excitement of the debaters, who to a great extent are the originators of and participants in never ending debates. As to the division of kingdoms and Christian states due to discords among themselves, although they unite against the Turks for this undertaking, nonetheless they easily return to disunity due to the diversity of aims and interests among themselves. Not to mention many princes and lords, and nations which cannot even unite either among themselves or with others, due to the variety of religions and sects in which they live which appal each other. Furthermore, the celibacy and monogamy that Christian law induces deprives the Republic of the number of people that it would produce.[44]

On the contrary, Marchesi gives a diametrically opposite picture of the Ottoman Empire:

> Those who went [to Turkey] say things to be the contrary among the Turks. Since they have a single religion, a single prince and a single government, and since there are few celibates among them and more so due to polygamy, they abound in numbers of people. Neither do they have artists or doers of superabundantly useless things, nor do they care excessively about the study of industries and vain things or about pomp or eating and drinking. They do not have scholars of letters or advocates or similar professors. Even if they have, debates among them are very few and short. However, they

---

[43] Marcello Marchesi, op. cit., 8 V.
[44] Marcello Marchesi, op. cit., 2R-3R.

dedicate themselves universally to the art of war and they engage their time and money in it.[45]

This idealised vision of the Ottoman Empire as a great monolithic 'war-machine' was extremely common among the Italians from the Renaissance onwards. One also sees examples from antiquity in Marchesi, again within a humanistic spirit, in accordance with the fashion of his times. He equates the civilised world with the Romans and the Turks with the Huns, the Parthians and the Saracens, and criticizes the Romans for having been incapable of adapting their military strategy to the 'chaotic' and 'undisciplined' manner of fighting of the barbarians.[46] It is a common theme of the writers of the Renaissance, which was carried well into the later centuries, to equate the 'civilised world' (i.e. Europe) with the Greeks and the Romans, and the barbarians with the eternal enemy of the Greeks, namely the Persians. This identification of the barbarian and alien 'other' continued with the Arabs from the eighth century onwards, and then with the Turks (i.e. the Ottomans) starting from the fifteenth century, with the milestone event being the fall of Constantinople on the 29th May 1453.

Marchesi seeks to persuade the reader that as there have been the great crusades of the past, an *offensive* war declared on the Turk *is* the only solution to saving Europe from these barbarians. He not only endorses the thereto existing necessary military and tactical suggestions to defeat the Ottomans, but also presents the reader with a valuable self-portrait of the European aristocracy and its lack of interest in taking any united action against their principal enemy. It is in a way curious that almost all the sources of the time lead one to conclude that, behind the rhetoric of the 'barbarian Turks', enmities among the Christian rulers exceeded the infidel threat. In this respect the Marchesi manuscript is not only a source of self-criticism, but also representative of the changing political milieu of seventeenth-century Europe, where the upcoming religious wars, coupled with the ever-present Ottoman threat, set the European political agenda. In fact, approximately two decades after Marchesi, another papal figure, Angelo Petricca da Sonnino, a representative of the *Propaganda Fide*, emphasised the same points in a somewhat different political vocabulary. Together with da Sonnino in 1640 and Fra Paolo da Lagni in 1679, as later will be shown, Marchesi and his successors within the pontifical milieu were the precursors of the idea of a realisable Christian alliance against the Turks, which was finalised under the auspices of Pope Innocent XI in the defence of Vienna in 1683.

---

[45] Marcello Marchesi, op. cit., 3R-3V.
[46] Marcello Marchesi, op. cit., 10R-10V.

Our second representative of pontifical policies from the seventeenth century vis-à-vis the Turks is Angelo Petricca da Sonnino. Our information on him comes mainly from the office that he held as 'vicar apostolic' in Istanbul, that is, as the representative of *Propaganda Fide* in the Ottoman Empire. *La Congregatione di Propaganda Fide* [The Congregation for the Propagation of Faith] was the institution of the pontificate designed to bring all the Catholic missions of the world under the centralised authority of Rome. The reasons for the establishment of the *Congregazione* were mainly twofold: one was to function as an agent of Counter-Reformation, the other was to counterbalance the authority of the other Catholic monarchs (i.e. Spain and Portugal) over the Catholic missions throughout the world. It was founded by Pope Gregory XV (1621-1623) in 1622, under the name of 'the Sacred Congregation' for the Propagation of Faith. As it became one of the most efficient institutions of the Holy See, all the Catholic missionary lands came under its jurisdiction in the Ottoman Empire, apart from those in Albania and the Greek islands.[47] The 'vicars apostolic' [*vicario apostolico*] as they were called, were directly responsible to the Pope, to fight the influence that the European monarchs had upon the missionaries protected by them, and therefore protecting their national interests. The congregation was founded on the idea that it was more advantageous to engage in missionary activities in Europe, rather than the peripheral Americas. This had the purpose of a *rapprochement* of the Catholic peoples with the Protestant and the Orthodox faiths, as well as the protection of the Maronites, and Armenians in the Ottoman territories.[48] More specifically, the aim of the *Propaganda Fide* in the Ottoman lands was to convert the Armenian and Orthodox Ottoman citizens as well as those of other Eastern rites to Catholicism. This, consequently, meant extending the sphere of influence of the Catholic Church in lands where the authority of the Pope was not recognised, making the Christian heretics once more accept the principle of *primatu papo*, as well as gaining allies from within the Ottoman state in the case of an eventual war against the Ottomans.

Angelo Petricca da Sonnino belonged to the Franciscan order (one of the most influential in the Ottoman Empire) and lived in Istanbul between 1636 and 1639. Charles A. Frazee refers to his memoirs, written in 1639, in which he 'claimed that [sultan] Murad IV [1612-1640] had lost control over the armed forces and that the

---

[47] Charles A. Frazee, *Catholics and Sultans. The Church and the Ottoman Empire. 1453-1923* (Bristol: Cambridge University Press, 1983), p.88.
[48] Giovanna Motta, 'Presenza ottomana tra Mediterraneo e centro-Europa: contrasti e reciproche influenze', in Gaetano Platania (ed.), *L'Europa centro-orientale e il pericolo turco tra sei e settecento. Atti del convegno internazionale (Viterbo, 23-25 Novembre 1998)*, (Viterbo: Sette Città, 2000), pp. 21-22.

opportunity was open for a united Christian Europe to push the Turks back into Asia.'[49] These memoirs probably refer to the collection of *relazioni,* written during his stay in Istanbul. Most probably, the *relazioni* were formed into the present treatise, parts of which appear below, and which he presented to Cardinal Antonio Barberino,[50] a most important patron of the idea of crusade himself, a year later, in 1640, da Sonnino dedicated his treatise to Cardinal Antonio Barberino and entitled it *Trattato del modo facile d'espugnare il Turco, e discacciarlo dalli molti Regni che possiede in Europa* [Treatise on the Easy Way of defeating the Turk, and of Expelling him from many Kingdoms that he Possesses in Europe]. It is dated 10th May 1640.[51]

He bases his treatise on four main arguments. The first point is the fact that the Ottomans had demolished most of the castles in the places that they conquered, therefore he says that the Christian army would have a great advantage in not having to besiege and try to conquer castles of the Turks. In a way he presents an almost surrealistic picture suggesting that the way to Istanbul was open to a marching Christian army without much military resistance from the Ottoman side. The second point da Sonnino strongly emphasises is the presence of Christian peoples within the Ottoman Empire. Evidently he sees the Christian peoples of the Ottoman Empire as potential allies, on whom one may count. For as he elaborates, 'the fathers would join up with the converted sons serving in the Turkish army' once a war starts between the Christians and Ottomans[52]. He says:

> The second point that deserves consideration to the same effect is that the Turkish state has many Christians as I have mentioned above, and although they are schismatic (that is to say disobedient to the High Roman Pontificate), according to my experience, this schism and this difference is limited in our times solely to the Greek prelates. Since people are now made uncouth and ignorant, as they are unable to discern these questions of *Primatu Papo,*[53] by seeing only a cross on the banners of the armies,

---

[49] Frazee, op. cit., p. 97. The memoir mentioned is: G. B. Cervellini (ed.), 'Relazioni da Costantinopoli del Vicario Patriarcale Angelo Petricca, 1636-39', *Bessarione,* XXVIII (1912).

[50] Cardinal Antonio Barberino belonged to the influential Barberini Family in Rome, who had himself as a youth written a treatise of war against the Turks.

[51] Angelo Petricca da Sonnino, *Trattato del modo facile d'espugnare il Turco, e discacciarlo dalli molti Regni che possiede in Europa. Composto dal padre Maestro Angelo Petricca da Sonnino Min: Conven: già Vicario Patriarcale di Constantinopoli, Commissario gn`le in Oriente, e Prefetto de Missionarij di Valacchia, et Moldavia. Dedicated to Cardinal Antonio Barberino. 10 Maggio 1640* (Città del Vaticano: Biblioteca Apostolica Vaticana: Barb. lat. 5151.).

[52] da Sonnino, op. cit., 5V.

[53] The recognition of primacy of the Pope amongst the other churches and authorities in Christendom.

> knowing that they are armies gathered under the name of Christ, they would run to unite with them.[54]

However, the general tone of the manuscript suggests, as da Sonnino himself later on explicitly states, that he would have preferred the conversion of the Christians of Eastern rites to the Catholic faith, as he mentions this wish of his not only for the Eastern Christians, but quite unrealistically also for the Turks.[55]

The third point is the consolidation of the Christian presence once the Ottoman lands are conquered. He puts forward his third point, in suggesting a rebuilding of castles in the lands taken back from the Turks, for the purpose of consolidation of the conquest. He suggests that the Christians of the conquered lands should not be harmed, and the people be treated as brothers, unlike the past examples of the Latin conquests of Byzantine lands as in the Fourth Crusade in 1204 where the Latin army conquered and sacked Constantinople, which was one of the main events contributing to the definite antagonism between Byzantium and the West, making the Constantinopolitans say: 'We prefer to see Turkish turbans in the city, rather than seeing Latin hats!'

The fourth and perhaps the most crucial point of the treatise is da Sonnino's open invitation to all the Christian rulers of Europe to go to war against the Turks. He considers the failure to do so as the biggest strategic and political mistake of all time against the infidels. The reason is that the only way to defeat the Sultan is to attack him from various sides, on land and on sea simultaneously, in order to divide his forces and prevent him from going to the battlefield personally, which would demoralise his soldiers.[56] The most crucial aspect of this move would be the unity of Christian princes at least during the Thirty Years War. As an example of overcoming differences between Christian nations, he gives the historical fact of the Fourth Crusade, where the French and Venetians joined to conquer Constantinople, ironically, against another Christian country. There is a strong reference to the Thirty Years War, as later on he suggests that the fighting Christian princes make at least a truce, if not peace, and making use of such a truce, direct their forces against the Turks.[57]

Considering these ideas contained in da Sonnino's work, having examined the realistic, as well as the unrealistic parts, one is left with two conclusions: either he was very ignorant of the strategic and military facts concerning the Ottoman Empire, as well as over-optimistic about the political ones, or the whole treatise must be considered in another light; namely, that of the political milieu in which the Holy

---

[54] da Sonnino, op. cit., 5R-5V.
[55] da Sonnino, op. cit., 18R.
[56] da Sonnino, op. cit., 9R-9V.
[57] da Sonnino, op. cit., 11R.

## The Genealogy of the 'Other': The Turks, Islam and Europe

See found itself towards the mid-seventeenth century, and in the midst of the Thirty Years War, after which almost half of Europe was lost to the Protestants. The years following his work saw the Treaty of Westphalia in 1648, and the consolidation of the Protestant states, as well as France's reassertion of its position within the European political system, a state with a Catholic majority but rarely in agreement with the Holy See, a state that did not hesitate to ally itself with Protestant Sweden to counter-balance the Catholic German presence in Europe. Under such conditions, the political vocabulary used by da Sonnino reflects the policy of Pope Urban VIII who tried in vain to settle the enmities between France and Spain, to ally them against the Protestants in the Thirty Years War. According to Eamon Duffy, 'The failure of the Pope to achieve peace between the Catholic parties to the Thirty Years War was an eloquent – and for the Papacy an ominous – indicator of the increasingly marginal place of religious considerations in determining the politics of Europe.'[58] This same aim of da Sonnino's to unite the Christian rulers against the Ottoman infidels, though proving to be a failure during the Thirty Years War, set an example for the future clergy and for Pope Innocent XI, and was successful in the long-term. It was a success not of papal policies to unite Europe in times of religious schism, but rather of military policies to expel the Ottoman military presence from Europe. In other words, 'to push the Turks back to where they came from', as it was often said.

However, da Sonnino's intention during the religious wars was precisely also a military one, which was to divert attention from the war in Europe onto the Ottomans by trying to create a completely different war front. This would have served a triple function: ending enmities between the Christians; defeating and conquering Ottoman lands, hence its riches; and finally reasserting the unifying and supreme ancient role of the Mother Church, at a time when the Europe of the modern era was drawing itself away towards another political system, which did not care much about European religious unity if it did not suit its interest. Although this was the case in relations among Christian states, when it came to dealing with the non-European Ottomans, unity under Christendom against the common enemy still mattered in the political rhetoric.

As far as the manuscripts of Marchesi and da Sonnino concern the 'Turkish Question' and an identity of 'Europeanness' built around Christendom and European unity, the following remarks may be made concerning the role of the papacy in relation to the Ottoman Empire in seventeenth-century Europe. There were two main means of confrontation and/or cooperation between the Italian states and the Ottomans, namely trade and war. Venice mainly tried to maintain trade relations with the Ottomans. As a general rule, when war brought more profit than trade, it

---

[58] Eamon Duffy, *Saints and Sinners. A History of the Popes* (Yale University Press, 1997), p. 184.

did not hesitate to take part in war. In such cases it presented itself as the most ardent advocate of war, as it was on the occasion of the naval battle of Lepanto in 1571. However, Venice normally saw profit in a peaceful co-existence with the Ottomans, as trade and war usually do not go together. The Veneto-Ottoman peace of 1479 and the fall of Otranto to the Ottomans in the following year was such an example, in spite of expectations of the feared Ottoman attack on Rome.

An important source of information about the image that the Turks enjoyed in this period is the *relazioni* of the Venetian ambassadors. They somehow present the historian with a different point of view concerning the military aspects of the Ottoman Empire than those coming from the clergy of Rome. This results from the substantial differences in the perceptions of the Ottoman Empire of Venice and Rome. As can be concluded from the *relazione* of the Venetian ambassador Alvise Contarini, who was the Venetian *bailo* residing in Istanbul at the time da Sonnino was there, for the Venetians, the Turks were a political and military entity to get along with as diplomatically as possible with minimum losses, possibly evading war at all costs, with the prime aim of maximising trade profits. For Rome, they were an entity to wage war upon at all costs, yet, ironically enough, it somehow could never be realised. It was the Venetian ambassador to Rome, Paolo Paruta, who, in 1594, opposed Clement VIII (1592-1605), who wanted to wage war against the Ottomans, taking advantage of the supposed weakness of the new sultan Murad III compared to his ancestors and the weakening effects of the long Turco-Persian war (1578-1590). It was Paruta's vision, seen from the Venetian perspective, that precisely because the Ottomans had emerged victorious from the Turco-Persian war, the counterbalancing effect of Persia was gone, and the best policy would be a wait-and-see one, instead of a new crusade which would be detrimental to the interests of the Italians.[59]

It seems that although da Sonnino was neither a diplomat nor an expert military strategist, he must have had some common sense to understand that the picture he gave in his treatise on the Ottoman Empire, and especially on its military aspects, was not totally realistic. The exaggerated image he presents the reader with about the military weaknesses of the Ottomans most reasonably stems from the ideological preoccupation of promoting a crusade against the Ottomans in an era of Catholic-Protestant clashes in Europe. It somehow sounds ironical to hear pleas for a crusade from an authority of the Catholic Church in the middle of the Thirty Years War, from a political point of view. However, it makes total sense from an ideological point of view to promote war against the infidels to divert attention from the heretic *Protestant* question to the *infidel* question, therefore achieving the twofold aim of transporting

---

[59] Giovanni Pillinini, 'Un discorso inedito di Paolo Paruta', in *Archivio Veneto*, LXXIV, (1964), pp. 7-8.

an essentially European war to a geographically remote area, and restoring the papacy to a unifying role at the heart of European politics. This was a role that was lost following the Reformation, after centuries of prestige for the papacy as the spiritual and partly also the temporal leader of Christendom. Therefore, the reinforcement of a European identity around *Christendom* found its expression in the seventeenth century in the efforts of the papacy to use the *Turkish Question* as a uniting factor. So much so that, the identification of the *infidel* question with the *heretic* one, and the unconditional legitimacy of such a 'just war' in a Marchesian sense, pursued for centuries by the papacy, was disputed by the famous humanist Erasmus of Rotterdam in his *Consultatio de bello Turcis inferendo* some seventy years before Marchesi.[60]

It may easily be presumed that once the crusade was realised, the 'war against the Turk' represented an excellent opportunity for Christendom, it would not only have presented a valuable acquisition in terms of wealth and land, but also temporary political unity in Christendom, or at least a truce in the middle of the Thirty Years War. On this, da Sonnino says: 'May God permit that the Christian arms join against the Turk. Moreover, if I am not mistaken, this would enable the easiest way to dictate to him at least a truce – if not peace – so that one can make peace among the princes for at least a few years, without a ceasefire.'[61] The feasibility of the task is illustrated by him giving the historical example of the crusader conquest of Constantinople in the Fourth Crusade in 1204. He says:

> Some would ask, 'Who would then bring agreement among the Christian princes once the Turk is defeated? They would fight among themselves and there would never be peace.' I would respond, who brought agreement between the French and the Venetians when they took Constantinople and the empire of the Greeks, as history speaks? With utmost peace the French remained the lords of Constantinople, and gave the patriarchate of the *terra firma* to the Venetians with the islands and other provinces. The empire of the French in Constantinople lasted around sixty years. In the future, many kingdoms occupied by the Turk in Europe could do like this.[62]

---

[60] Erasmus of Rotterdam, ed. A.G. Weiler, 'Utilissima consultatio de bello Turcis inferendo', in *Opera omnia Desiderii Erasmi Roteordami* (Amsterdam, New York, Oxford and Tokyo, 1969–), III, 1-8, at 52-56, 68-71, 74, 81-82, in Norman Housley, (ed. and trans.), *Documents on the later crusades 1274-1580*, (London, 1996), pp. 178-183.

[61] da Sonnino, op. cit., p. 11R.

[62] da Sonnino, op.cit., pp. 8 V-9 R

In this respect da Sonnino's overemphasis of the similarities between the Greeks and the Latins from a religious point of view and his total deliberate neglect of the Protestant opposition as far as religious diversities are concerned, serve his aim of diverging attention from internal European problems to a different geographical area. It seems that the Turks almost served as an outlet of expression by being the *other* and the *disapproved of,* in the mind of the Europeans. As to the significance of this new seventeenth-century interpretation of the concept of crusade, Norman Housley writes:

> Until a few years ago most historians would have said that the inclusion of a chapter on events in the sixteenth century in a book about the later crusades was at best superfluous, and at worst misguided. They would have argued that popular and governmental commitment to a crusade against the Turks was negligible by 1500; that calls for a crusade, no matter how frequently or forcefully made by individual enthusiasts or the papal Curia, were therefore anachronistic, meriting serious study only by antiquarians; and most importantly, that narrating the great conflicts which occurred in the sixteenth century between the Ottomans and their western enemies, especially the Habsburgs, in terms of a religious war is as misleading as applying that description to, say, the allied campaigns against the Turkish armies in the First World War. It is the achievements of Professor K.M. Setton to have shown how inaccurate this view was...[63] By simply describing what took place, Professor Setton demonstrated that, while these relations accommodated many new features characteristic of an age of profound change, they also formed a continuation of crusading history, in terms of basic ideas and institutions as well as terminology. No great chasm separated the world of King Philip II of Spain and Pope Pius V from that of Philip the Good of Burgundy and Pius II; the one evolved from the other and shared many of its features. [64]

As a milestone, the battle of Nicopolis (Niğbolu) in Bulgaria on 25<sup>th</sup> September 1396 against the Ottomans was a turning point for the crusaders where the great enthusiasm of the past to reconquer the Holy Lands and Eastern Europe was lost for good.[65] The fall of Constantinople made the Europeans realise a fact that was gradually, but

---

[63] On the ideas of Setton, see Kenneth M. Setton, *The Papacy and the Levant (1204-1571),* Vol. II. (Philadelphia: The American Philosophical Society, 1978).

[64] Norman Housley, *The Later Crusades. From Lyons to Alcazar, 1274-1580* (Oxford: Oxford University Press: 1992), p. 118.

[65] Aziz S. Atiya, *Crusade, Commerce and Culture* (Bloomington: Indiana University Press, 1962), p. 110.

rapidly emerging in Eastern Europe: that the Ottomans possessed almost the entire Balkans. The various incursions of the Ottomans in Friuli in the late 1460s and the 1470s, followed by the fall of Otranto in 1480, only impressed upon the Italian mind the urgent necessity to defend at least the homeland. For Rome, the period between the fall of Constantinople and the Reformation of the early sixteenth century was a time of attempts to organise various crusades to save Christendom from the infidel Turks. Beginning with the Reformation and followed by the Thirty Years War, the Turkish question was planned to be solved simultaneously with the Protestant question. This was either in the form of targeting the Protestants with exhortations to war against the Turks, as seen in the Marchesi manuscript, or in the form of an ideological Counter-Reformation rhetoric, or in the terms of the 'unity of Christendom' rhetoric, to take united military action with the Protestants against the Turks in order to shift the military conflict between the Protestants and the Catholics onto the Ottoman lands, as seen in the da Sonnino manuscript. As Aldobrandino Malvezzi documents in his book *L'Islamismo e la Cultura Europea*, Dupreau in 1605 wrote: 'In these times of ours, Mohammedanism was revived by Luther and by his disciples' and as Lodovico Maracci wrote in 1689: 'The Calvinists and the Sacramentalists are both sons and disciples of Mohammedans.'[66]

## The post-Vienna Phase and the 'Innocuous' Turk of the Enlightenment

It was only after 1683 that it became evident to the Europeans that the Turks had neither the willingness nor the military capacity to undertake a conquest of the whole of Europe anymore, let alone that of Rome and becoming the masters of *Roma caput mundi*. However, Italians still believed on the eve of 1683 that a Turkish attack on Rome was imminent. International politics concerning the Ottomans were partly determined after 1683 by the internal weaknesses of the Ottomans towards the turn of the seventeenth century. The new European balance of power and relative stability of the Westphalian system, achieved after decades of Protestant-Catholic conflict in 1648, was coupled with the consolidation of the power of the old nation states such as France and England. Furthermore, the extension of European sovereignty to the newly conquered colonies outside Europe also gradually opened an era where the European questions were now transported to, and fought in the world at large. This not only prepared the ground for the more favourable romantic image of the Turk, but it also created a tangible change in the European attitude towards the Turkish question. The 'Turk' in the Age

---

[66] Aldobrandino Malvezzi, *L'Islamismo e la Cultura Europea* (Firenze: Sansoni Editore, 1956), p. 260.

of Enlightenment continued to be the antithesis of the European civilisation. It is not a coincidence that orientalism in the modern sense was born and became a part of the European perception of the Orient in this period. In fact, the Ottoman question never became an issue of a 'total crusade of Christendom' after the beginning of the eighteenth century, needless to say, which ruled out single military clashes between the Ottomans and the European powers. It returned to the agenda on the eve of the First World War in a different political vocabulary, not under the name of 'crusade' anymore, but under the rhetoric of the 'sick man of Europe'. This was a period of exhaustion in the colonial wars of the European powers, and once again a short-lived period of carrying the familiar refrain of the 'civilised world' against the old 'despots'.

The literary works of the Venetians dared consider the civilised aspects of the Ottomans only after the failure in Vienna. The *tremendous invincible* image of the Turk following the fall of Constantinople, altered as a result of the joint Christian victory in Lepanto to the *vincible Turk*. This was followed by absorbing the *Turk* in the European mind in the coming decades after the Ottoman failure in Vienna in 1683, as the now *innocuous Turk* of the eighteenth century. It then culminated in the second half of the nineteenth century in the image of the *sick man of Europe*. It is after this *innocuous Turk* phase that we see the Venetians starting to write about an image of the Turk that was to produce in the eighteenth-century Venetian literature (particularly after the Treaty of Passarowitz in 1718) themes of interest about the daily and cultural life of the Turks not spoilt by themes 'directly tied to war-matters or inspired by visceral hatred.'[67] In *Della Letteratura de' Turchi*,[68] Giovanni Battista Donado (also known as Giambattista Donà) could be considered to herald such a future in Venetian literature on the Turks. The year 1688, the year *Della Letteratura de' Turchi* was published, was shortly after the defeat of Vienna, and is on the eve of the *romanticisation* of the Orient and the appearance of the Ottoman Empire as the home of oriental mystery and the *feminine Orient*.[69] The transforming importance of the second siege of Vienna in the European attitude towards the Ottomans is expressed by Kenneth Setton as follows:

---

[67] Paolo Preto, 'Il mito del Turco nella letteratura veneziana', in Carlo Pirovano (ed.), *Venezia e i Turchi. Scontri e confronti di due civiltà* (Milano: Electa Editrice, 1985), p. 136.
[68] Giovanni Battista Donado, *Della Letteratura de' Turchi* (Venetia: Per Andrea Poletti, 1688).
[69] Petra Kappert, 'From Romanticisation to colonial dominance: Historical changes in European perception of the Middle East', in J. Hippler ve A. Lueg (ed.), *The Next Threat. Western Perceptions of Islam* (London, 1995).

> No episode in the history of Europe in the seventeenth century has attracted more attention than the second Turkish siege of Vienna. The centenary 'remembrance of things past' in 1983 as well as in 1883 has produced an abundance of literature on the subject.[70]

It is around this time that Giambattista Donà makes his appearance in the literature on the Ottoman Empire. Donà was elected as ambassador to Constantinople on 19th May 1680. In 1683, he was called back to Venice for exceeding his authority as an ambassador for he was suspected of having made secret agreements with the Ottomans. Later, his innocence was proved. Donà read his *relazione* on his mission to Constantinople in the Venetian senate on 20th August 1684. His *relazione* remains the last one until the peace of Karlowitz.[71] According to Setton, Donà enjoyed close relations with the Grand Vizier Kara Mustafa Paşa from 1682, for it was in the latter's interest to maintain close relations with Venice because of his plan to attack the Habsburgs, 'bestowing gifts upon Donà',[72] and also given that there had been peace between Venice and the Ottomans for more than a decade, which was not to be disturbed on the eve of the second siege of Vienna, which was to come the following year.[73] The *Della Letteratura de' Turchi* of Giambattista Donà:

> had a great, though an ephemeral success, because evidently after centuries of *Turquesque* publicity obsessed by the monotony of themes of the Crusade, the wickedness, barbarities and ferocity of the Turks, many received this book with a sigh of relief, though with inadequate means of understanding the literary patrimony of a nation which was believed to be unable to express itself as a valid and autonomous civilisation.[74]

The term 'inadequate means of understanding the literary patrimony of a nation' used by Paolo Preto in the above quotation alludes to the fact that Giambattista Donà was neither a man of letters nor a philologist by profession. He admits to having learned some Turkish in Venice before departing for his *bailaggio* in Istanbul; however, neither his linguistic skills nor the time he had for undertaking such a work as

---

[70] Kenneth M. Setton, *Venice, Austria and the Turks in the Seventeenth Century* (Philadelphia: The American Philosophical Society, 1991), p. 260.
[71] Nicolò Barozzi and Guglielmo Berchet, *Le Relazioni degli stati europei lette al Senato dagli Ambasciatori Veneziani nel Secolo Decimosettimo. Turchia.*, Volume unico-Parte I. (Venezia: Prem. Stabil. Tip. di P. Naratovich Edit., 1871), p. 7.
[72] Kenneth M. Setton, *Venice*, op. cit., p. 257.
[73] ibid.
[74] Paolo Preto, *Venezia e i Turchi* (Firenze: G. C. Sansoni Editore, 1975), p. 345.

*Della Letteratura de' Turchi* was adequate. Donà was a diplomat and a politician by profession. He served in Venice as the member [*savio*] of the Council of Venice, was appointed to the difficult task of ambassador to Constantinople in 1680, was then called back to Venice in 1684 and incarcerated for an alleged conspiracy to reach secret agreements with the Ottomans, specifically of having caused Venice to pay too high a sum of money as reparations for the damages caused to the Ottomans in 1682 by the quasi-Venetian subjects of Dalmatia, the Morlacchi. After his innocence was proved, his membership to the council was restored to him, and he died in 1700, at the age of seventy-six.[75]

It is within this historical context that Donà's book should be read. He had an inquisitive mind and his book should not be considered as the scholarly work of an expert on the subject, but rather as a pioneering work that attempts to eradicate the negative image of the Turk in Venice and elsewhere as an uncouth man, which prevailed until the 1680s. The preface to his book was written by the dragoman of the Venetian embassy in Istanbul, Gian Rinaldo Carli and Pietro Donà, the son of the author. In the book it is written that G. Donà made Gian Rinaldo Carli do the translations of the material he used for his book. Carli belonged to a noble Dalmatian family from Koper and had stayed for at least fifty years in the Ottoman Empire following the fall of Candia in Crete. Many interpreters of the Italian language who worked in the Ottoman Empire between the sixteenth and the eighteenth centuries were from Dalmatia.[76] The preface to *Della Letteratura de' Turchi* is as follows:

> Of the vast empire of the Turks, which extends itself to a major part of Asia, Africa and Europe, many have described the countries, the nations and the traditions, not to mention the political government of the great court of the Ottoman monarchs. It is the curiosity of the French writers[77] who have surpassed the Italians and the Germans with minute diligence, that described all the sects of their religions, very sacred ceremonies, as well as the profane ones, the differences of dress of women as well as men, the civil laws and offices as well as the military ones, and the various and diverse emblems of their dignitaries, which to a major extent consist of the various and different

---

[75] Nicolò Barozzi and Guglielmo Berchet, op. cit., p. 292.

[76] [http://www.zrs-kp.si/Zaloznistvo/acta/pov5013.htm]

[77] Probably the first name that comes to one's mind is the famous Frenchman Guillaume Postel (born in 1510), or Guglielmo Postello (as he was called in Venice), whose name is inseparable from that of Venice. The manuscripts that he obtained in his travels in the Orient are today in the San Marco Library of Venice. Postel, whose first travel commenced in the year 1536, stayed also in Istanbul, looking for books in Chaldean. See Marion Leathers Kuntz, 'L'Orientalismo di Guglielmo Postello e Venezia', in Lionello Lanciotti (ed.), *Venezia e l'Oriente* (Firenze: Leo S. Olschki Editore, 1987).

forms of their caps and turbans. However, of the study of the literature of the Turks, no or very little news until now has been disclosed in Europe. Moreover, the universal, or rather, the erroneous idea was diffused that the Turkish Nation was indeed ignorant of the good and fine letters, incapable of rhetoric, of poetry and were remote from the study of law, medicine, philosophy and mathematics and that it was solely devoted to the use of arms. Since military discipline and the art of war have been the areas where the Turks have made themselves excellent and terrible, they occupied, thanks to their victories, many kingdoms and provinces of Christian princes and of other neighbouring sects of theirs.[78] Therefore, within a range of a hundred and fifty years, six eminent authors undertook to teach the Christian princes the way to beat them in war and really to expel them from Europe. These were Gilenio Busbeqio[79] and Francesco Savaro, the lord of Breves [Bresse in France?], both of them ambassadors, the former, that of the Emperor [*Cesare*], the latter, that of the King of France [*Re Christianissimo*] to the Porte. One wrote in Latin on the strategy of resisting and waging war against the Turk, the other one wrote a book in the French language on the secure means of destroying the Ottoman monarchy. Subsequently, the same matter was cleverly treated by the lord of Nue in the French language, and by Lazzaro Soranzo[80] in Italian in the book *Imperio Ottomano* [The Ottoman Empire] and by Achille Tarducci in the discourse entitled *Il Turco vincibile in Ungaria con mediocri aiuti di Germania* [The Vincible Turk in Hungary with the moderate aid of Germany]. Lastly the learned Giobbo Ludolfo [Hiob Ludolf, 1624-1704], counsellor of the Holy Imperial Majesty, in the book that he wrote, *De bello contra Turcas feliciter conficiendo* [How to Successfully Conduct War against the Turks], teaches with extremely fine politics, the means of really extinguishing the Turkish Religion in Europe and of conserving and maintaining the kingdoms and provinces in obedience which have been taken away from the barbarians with the last victories. Therefore, there not being anyone to take care of researching the study and the literature of the Turks, the senator of eminent judgement, of firm letters and of notable eloquence, Giovanni Battista Donado, in the conspicuous

---

[78] The allusion here is to the Shiites.
[79] O.G. de Busbeq, *The Turkish Letters*, E. Forster (ed.), (Oxford: 1968.) See also Zweder von Martels, 'Impressions of the Ottoman Empire in the Writings of Augerius Busbequius (1520/1-1591)', *Journal of Mediterranean Studies*, (Malta), Vol. 5, No. 2, (1995), pp. 209-221.
[80] See Lazzaro Soranzo, op. cit. It is alluded to the same Lazzaro Soranzo and his work mentioned earlier in the article.

office of bailo in Constantinople for the Most Serene Republic of Venice, gave all the signs of extreme prudence, of invincible perseverance and of unmatchable zeal towards his country, who, more than anyone else, was able to grasp secret notices with shrewd diligence from the Turkish Empire: the illustrious *relazione* on the sciences of the Turks, which he wrote to his Monsignor brother the Abbot. I – knowing what a pity it would have been if it had stayed buried in private hands – have implored His Excellency [Donà's brother] not to envy such rare curiosity of the men of letters and important knowledge. As a result of his benign concession, which gave honour to my printers, the learned curiosity of your erudite intelligence will be nourished, O Reader. May you live happily.[81]

The preface of the book is followed by the introduction of Donà in the form of a letter to his brother Abbot Andrea, where he gives a wide range inventory of literary and scientific patrimony of the Ottomans. Donà continues

> However, you, my brother *signore*, should know that, despite the above information, one should not think all Turks to be in possession of arts and sciences, since most of them are deprived of publications and are compelled to a forced ignorance. However, there are various concrete pieces of evidence of the not-mediocre cognition of letters and of intelligence, most of which are in positive terms.
>
> The necessity of teaching the Qur'an [*Alcorano*] for the purpose of their own instruction as well as for other reasons, very easily give reason not to fall into the universal error that they are totally ignorant.
>
> To be able to understand this truth better, however, one should consider that the Turkish language is like it is in provincial Italy, where every person speaks with the forms, the pronunciation and the accent of his own locality. However it [Turkish] becomes embellished by Persian, as we do with the Tuscan language.

---

[81] The translation of the passages from the book *Della letterature de'Turchi* of Donà and the page numbers are taken from the copy found in the Biblioteca Universitaria of Padua, and due to printing inadequacies of the time, there may occur – as it sometime does – shifts in page numbers or minuscule differences in the text, when compared with other copies of the book even when printed by the same publisher.

## The Genealogy of the 'Other': The Turks, Islam and Europe

However, there will be more proof of this matter. Likewise, also Arabic is present among the Turks, like Latin among us. Since the Qur'an is written in the mentioned language, Arabic becomes necessary for them, as would be to us the language in which the Holy Scriptures are written. They use the entire Arabic manners, voices, and periods for ornament, eloquence and decor mostly in the schemes and commandments, and other orders of major transactions and arbiters; letters of the prince, ministers, *paşas* [*Bassà*] and the command of the imperial will. As a result, the major erudition among them is explained and is present in the men of law, who are those who are employed in the tribunals of the judiciary, in the parishes or clergy of theirs, as said; as well as in the most distinguished men of the court of the notaries, secretaries and chancellors, all of which for the sake of necessity of their office understand, speak and write Arabic. It is well-known how much these arts and sciences have been explained by Arab authors, whose entire works are found a long time among the Turks in their original character and language.[82]

Sufficient and evident proof of this comes from a book entitled: *Rudimento della Lingua Turchesca* [Rudiments of the Turkish Language] written by the Armenian Signor D. Giovanni Agaup, born in Constantinople, published in Venice in the year 1685, dedicated to you my brother, Signor Andrea, the abbot, for your pious employment at the house of catechumens, where the Turkish language is taught with all the grammatical rules, as they do in the above mentioned City of Constantinople.[83]

To strengthen this matter further, it is witnessed that the sultans have from time to time, erected various schools, many colleges and lecture houses, also at the level of doctorate to qualify the men at the judiciary, and especially those serving at mosques and to regulate the consciences of the priests in charge, or others, especially to train them for the pulpit on which they climb particularly at feasts, preaching to the people where they seek to teach the moral virtues, the detestation of vices and the reverence and adoration of the supreme Deity. However, in order to give an example, I resolve to record here that which Hüseyin Efendi [*Hussein Effendi*] writes in his treatise *Della Grandezza della Casa Ottomana* [Of the Grandeur of the House of Osman], written in Constantinople.[84]

---

[82] Giovanni Battista Donado, *Della Letteratura de'Turchi* (Venetia: Per Andrea Poletti, 1688), pp. 5-8.
[83] Giovanni Battista Donado, op. cit., p. 10.
[84] Giovanni Battista Donado, op. cit., pp. 11-12.

The Hüseyin Efendi mentioned here is Hüseyin Hezârfen, born in İstanköy and died on 24th September 1691 in Istanbul. The translation reported here by Donà is the first part of the greater work Hüseyin Hezarfen wrote, entitled *Telhīs ül-beyān fī kavānīn-i āl-i Osmān*, about the laws of Mehmet IV, the first part being about the origins of the Ottoman dynasty, their family trees and order of succession to the throne. We learn from Babinger that Hüseyin Hezârfen met many European travellers and was eager to share with them his library and knowledge.[85] Hence one could assume that it was Donà's personal ties with Hüseyin Hezârfen that made him quote from Hezârfen's book extensively between pages 12 and 43 and 89 and 92 in *Della Letteratura de' Turchi*. The translation from Hüseyin Hezârfen's book starts with a short introduction about the beginning, the origins and the deeds of the first members of the House of Osman. Donà inserts bits and pieces from various chapters of Hüseyin Hezârfen's book, reaching as far as the time of the Valide Sultan (Mother Sultan) between pages 12 and 17. She was then alive and had given orders for the building of a mosque in the year 1663. This is followed by other translations from chapters on the hierarchy among the *ulema*, on pages 17 to 43. After these, Donà goes on to explain his selection and/or collection of books in different disciplines of letters and sciences starting from grammar and following with poetry and logic, mathematics, geometry and the like. Some of the books listed by Donà are as follows. In grammar, the listed books are the *Torch of Grammar* [*Lucerna Grammaticale*] by an anonymous author; An Arabic, Persian, Turkish and Chaldean dictionary, whose authors are not mentioned; *Rudiments of Turkish Grammar* [*Rudimenti della Grammatica Turca*], written, according to Donà, by Andrea di Ryer, who was the consul of the King of France to Egypt, published in Paris in 1633.[86]

In poetry, Donà says that there are numerous authors. *Compendium of Poetry* [*Summario di Poesia*], written by Hâfız Şirazî (Alfez Scirazì); *Compendium of Persian* [*Summario in Persiano*] by Fuzuli (Fesulì); *Compendium of Poetry* [*Summario di Poesia*], by Baki (Bachì); *Compendium of the Acts of Christ* [*Summario de' fatti di Christo*], in praise of his heroic actions by Nesîmî (Nascimì); *History* by Kassan Seham; *History* by the Patriarch Josef (Gioseffo Patriarca); *The Loves of Putifar* [*Amori di Putifar*], and *Iusul Ezeliche* (Yûsuf u-Zalîha).[87] Donà claims the discipline of logic to be the instrument for the rest of the sciences. He claims that various types of argumentation, all of which are to be found in the book *Introduction*

---

[85] Franz Babinger, *Osmanlı Tarih Yazarları ve Eserleri*, trans. Coşkun Üçok, (Ankara: Kültür ve Turizm Bakanlığı, 1982), pp. 251-255.
[86] Donà, op. cit. pp. 45-46.
[87] ibid., pp. 46-47.

## The Genealogy of the 'Other': The Turks, Islam and Europe

*to Logic* [*Isahuugì*] by an unmentioned author, are present in this discipline.[88] In mathematics, the author enumerates a book of speculative and practical arithmetic by Ali Kuşçu ( ? -1474) (Alì Alcusì); a book of geometry by Abialvafa; another book of general geometry by Aflinio; and *De Ponderibus* by Iranī.[89] In geometry, a book of Euclid's; in optics, a book of Ptolemy's; and in music the books of Alfasatì and Abisalifà among a few others are mentioned.[90]

Details of the books listed in all the disciplines by Donà are beyond the confines of this study; however, the examples mentioned will be sufficient to give the reader an idea about the way the author treats the subject in his book. However, the rest of the disciplines mentioned with occasional citations of some translated books are optics, music, medicine, chemistry, astrology, astronomy, philosophy, law, history, geography and prose.[91]

Donà, after having mentioned various authors in various subjects, writes that he wants to give a translated extract from the introduction of the history book written by Hüseyin Efendi [Cusseino Effendì], entitled: *Of the Grandeur of the Ottoman Empire* [*Delle grandezze dell'Imperio Ottomano*], alluding to the aforementioned book by Hüseyin Hezârfen, *Telhīs ül-beyān fī kavānīn-i āl-i Osmān*. He repeats the recurrent theme that the Turks are generally not as intelligent as the Venetians, and that they do not possess knowledge of sciences as much as *they* do.[92] This is followed by the translation from Hüseyin Hezârfen's book about the grandeur of the Ottoman Empire, which goes on for three pages in the tone of an ode and which was written during the reign of Mehmet IV. The author states that the reason why he has included this translation in the book is his conversations with 'the famous and most knowledgeable' Ifes Effendì. Donà mentions to Ifes Effendì his intentions of writing a book on the Ottomans and shows him another book by himself entitled *Of the History of Princes of the Past* [*Dell'Historie de' principi passati*]. It was written on the princes of *Kina* [China], and Ifes Effendì urges him to write another book on the Ottoman sultans so that it sets an example for European writers to write something decent and positive about the Ottomans. Donà writes that upon this encouragement by Ifes Effendì, he composed the present book entitled: *The Story of Greatness of the Ottoman Emperors* [*Racconto della grandezza degli imperatori ottomani*].[93] At this point, it must be said that it is not really clear whether he alludes to *Della Letteratura*

---

[88] ibid., pp. 47-48.
[89] ibid., p.48
[90] ibid., pp .48-49.
[91] ibid., pp. 49-88.
[92] ibid., p. 88.
[93] ibid., pp. 92-93.

63

*de' Turchi* or whether there was another book written by him entitled *Racconto della grandeza degli imperatori ottomani*. However, the former is more plausible.

In Donà's book there is also a list of translations of sayings in Turkish.[94] Some of them are reproduced here, with Donà's original transcription in italics:

> *Nè Kader giad idersèm bir muradè*
> *Nassib olmas mucaderden ziadè*
> However much one would strive for an end
> One would not receive anything more than what is predestined
>
> *Arefsen bir chiul ieter*
> *coriatsen ghir barghia (sic.)*
> For the man of understanding a rose is enough to smell
> An uncouth person [on the other hand] enters a garden to demolish it
>
> *Bir tazì ichì taussan birde totamas*
> A hunting dog cannot catch two rabbits at a time
>
> *Aref ssiad olur bu giaanè gam checher*
> *Giaael hamisè nessad olaimder è sem secher*[95]
> A man of understanding, in his struggle for happiness in this world, misses happiness and grieves.

The reader learns from the book that there was another work to be eventually published by Padua's Seminary Press, founded by Cardinal Gregorio Barbarigo, containing five hundred Turkish proverbs.[96]

As well as giving the translations of some religious orations for the month of Ramadan and a brief explanation on the matter of religious orations, translations of letters in Turkish are also given as examples. After this, one arrives at the subject of poetry among the Turks:

> Poetry is also very abundantly practised among the Turks. Here I do not write their rules of composition. However, they also have, like us, measure, harmony and dissonance, with which they express feelings with thoughts, and concepts with eloquence. They receive from Persian the gallantry of the

---

[94] ibid. pp. 97-100.
[95] ibid., pp. 97-98.
[96] ibid., p. 100.

## The Genealogy of the 'Other': The Turks, Islam and Europe

> word, as we receive from Tuscan, or rather from Sienese;[97] and from Arabic, as we do from Latin, they receive the power of the juicy and decorous way of speaking. They boast of some fables from which, as a result, one can understand what they mean. I have, however, had the following translated, since I did not take more time to examine further. For those who want to entirely satisfy their curiosity, there is an infinity of books in verse, most of which are in Persian, written in various meters and in strophe, and with harmony of rhyme, and they distinguish themselves very well, in the measure they were praised from other rhymes and figures, as men not so uncouth.[98]

Donà warns the reader that by translating the poetry, much is lost and that it loses its 'vagueness and often its juice, as do the new-born flowers that are transplanted, which do not have the colour, or beauty or odour they had before.'[99] Subsequently, the author gives examples of Turkish songs and comments on the music with which the lyrics are accompanied, as well as giving translations of songs into Italian.[100] A song with its musical notes and lyrics in Turkish transcribed in Italian characters is given in the appendix to the book.

Despite all these examples in Donà's book showing that the Turks were no longer barbarians and that they had all the elements of erudition necessary to qualify them as a civilised nation, Donà cannot help making the following remark, as an attempt to show that the conquered lands of the Europeans had their share in civilising the Turks:

> Having had the aforementioned things collected, I suppose that you will have from the reading of these notes, sufficient cognition that the Turkish Nation is no more buried in that brutal roughness, as it was before. Also this empire, as it is in the habit of the conquerors, in expanding its dominion and in introducing itself into the most beautiful provinces, conquered also gifts and fine arts, which the lands gradually conquered by it enjoyed.[101]

---

[97] The Tuscan dialect of Italian was gradually adopted as the standard Italian, starting from Dante Alighieri. In this process, the works of Dante Alighieri and Petrarch were of paramount importance. Although the Tuscan dialect is generally considered to be the standard Italian, presumably for its proximity to Latin, the Sienese (ie. Siena) dialect was traditionally considered to be the purest among the other dialects of Tuscany.

[98] Donà, op.cit., pp. 125-126. See also Mustafa Soykut, 'Della Letteratura de' Turchi'den Giovanni Battista Donado', in Mehmet Kalpaklı (ed.), *Osmanlı Divan Şiiri Üzerine Metinler* (İstanbul: Yapı Kredi Yayınları, 1999).

[99] Donà, op. cit. p. 130.

[100] ibid., pp. 134-135.

[101] Giovanni Battista Donado, op. cit., p. 135.

On the other hand, it convincingly results from the text that this passage is also the harbinger of the fact that the image enjoyed by the *Turk* in Venice was gradually undergoing a change after the failure in Vienna in 1683.

Donà's conviction and ideas about the subject matter of his book continue in the same way in his *relazione*, which attests to a change in the image that the Turks had enjoyed until then. However, he is still convinced about the nature and scope of the presence of erudition among the Turks, as this nature pertains not to erudition and culture for its sake. Rather, all the *medreses*, schools, reading of books and building of universities are seen as an effort by the sultans to keep their subjects under control. As his *relazione* to the Venetian Senate reads, upon his return to Venice in 1684, all these cultural facilities were seen by the sultans as necessary 'to keep the people in peace and order thanks to the judiciary, therefore it was *convenient* to back up erudition and study, and to *tolerate* the *diffusion of a mediocre cultivation of the mind.*'[102] However, as he continues in his *relazione*, now that he admits *at least a fragment of culture and study* among the Turks (and even that much was not admitted by the Venetian public opinion before him) he says that this natural faculty of the soul which craves for knowledge enables the Turks to discover that the prophet of their religion (Muhammad) was a fraud, and that he was destined to perish as a consequence of his lies. Donà adds that the Turks do not really have a religion and that although seen from outside they profess the *Muslim religion*, they confound its laws, which are already badly written.[103] Considering the selection of works pertaining to the letters and sciences of the Ottomans enumerated in his book, one can assert that his selection is not the result of meticulous research on the subject. It is rather a dilettante's *bricolage* in an early attempt in the study of Turcology. However, it should be acknowledged that 'Donà and his circle achieved at the end of the (seventeenth) century a cultural operation of great magnitude, suggesting for the first time to the Venetian public a new and an original way of approaching Turkish civilisation, for the first time studied in terms of its own values, which the West still has to discover.'[104]

Nevertheless, considering the pioneering nature of Donà's work, as well as the fact that he was by profession an ambassador in the Ottoman Empire and not a philologist, his work deserves a great deal of appreciation and attention, not for the quality of information or documentation but rather because it is the first example that reveals to the Venetian public that the Ottomans were not the bestial creatures they were believed to be but at least cultured people, however mediocre and inadequate the scope of their culture may have been.

---

[102] Nicolò Barozzi and Guglielmo Berchet, op. cit., pp. 295-296.
[103] ibid. p. 297.
[104] Paolo Preto, *Venezia e i Turchi* (Firenze: G. C. Sansoni Editore, 1975), p. 351.

In general, none of the authors mentioned in the present essay were marginal characters whose works had a limited and marginal audience at their times. On the contrary, most of them were authors of remarkable importance in their times, some of them even celebrities within the intellectual circles in which they were read, not to mention the even more renowned names such as Bessarion and Pope Pius II. These authors, some of whom are almost entirely forgotten today, not only gradually helped to create the image of the Turk in Italy as well as in Europe in their times, but were also the *formers of contemporary public opinion*, an opinion whose echoes and influences still linger in the present day in the form of defining the 'other' with characteristics as opposed to one's own.

Although pioneers of modern Turcology like Donà tried to eradicate a profound centuries-old ignorance and prejudice against the Turks, these images of the Turks persist to the present day. Even a famous historian of our century like Franz Babinger, whose valuable contributions to the study of Ottoman-Italian relations cannot be denied, was not free of the prejudices that the Italians held about the Turks some hundred years before him. One example, and not an atypical one, is his article '*Maometto il Conquistatore e gli umanisti d'Italia*'[105], an exposé in the form of an article about the alleged 'humanist' traits and the contacts that Mehmet II the Conqueror had with the Italian humanists. In Renaissance Europe, which was the age of rediscovery and the reinterpretation of Greco-Roman antiquity, the Europeans identified themselves with the rediscovered ancient Greece. The Ottomans, on the other hand, were identified with the eternal enemies of Greek civilisation, their antithesis: the Persians. The Ottomans therefore became the antithesis of the European civilisation. In Babinger's words:

> All that mattered to Mehmet II was to know the means and methods that enabled the great characters of antiquity – Alexander the Great, Xerxes, Caesar, Ptolemy – to realise their conquests. However, that which his western mentors had not taught him was the fact that the impetuous current of events always consigns wars and political successes, victories and failures to oblivion, while transforming through time and space the deeds and creations of the human spirit.[106]

---

[105] Franz Babinger, 'Maometto il Conquistatore e gli umanisti d'Italia', in *Aufsaetze und Abhandlungen zur Geschichte Suedosteuropas und der Levante*, Franz Babinger (Muenchen: Dr. Dr. Rudolf Trofenik, 1976.)

[106] Franz Babinger, 'Maometto il Conquistatore e gli umanisti d'Italia', in *Aufsaetze und Abhandlungen zur Geschichte Suedosteuropas und der Levante*, Franz Babinger (Muenchen: Dr. Dr. Rudolf Trofenik, 1976), p. 293.

These words of the famous historian of Turco-Italian relations Babinger, almost echo the travel account of Bassano who lived four hundred years before him. The Italian traveller Luigi Bassano, whose book *I Costumi et i Modi Particolari de la Vita de' Turchi* [The Customs and Particular Ways of Life of the Turks] was published in Rome in 1545, depicts the general populace of Istanbul as follows:

> The Turks do not have much intricacy of erudition and jurists... As soon as their children have learned to read and to write, they take them away from school. And the child who is able to do this well is accompanied into the city by all the other children of his school who chant odes to him. His disposition, proudly vain in front of all, encourages the other children to compete to learn as soon as possible, in order to be accompanied and honoured with the same chants.[107]

This selective interpretation of history of some of the modern historians results from the renowned work of the Venetian abbot Giambattista Toderini's *Letteratura Turchesca,* published in 1787, which was one of the most comprehensive and authoritative works of Turcology of its time, one hundred years after the pioneering work of Donà. In the introduction, Toderini says:

---

[107] M. Luigi da Zara Bassano, *I Costumi et i Modi Particolari de la Vita de' Turchi*, Roma: n.p., 1545, facsimile edition by Franz Babinger, (Monaco di Baviera: Casa Editrice Max Hueber, 1963), p. 37 recto. It must not go unmentioned that there is a striking similarity between the image of the Turk as depicted by Europeans and the image of the Muslims of India as having been martial oppressors of the Hindus for centuries. On this subject see the beginning of the 19th century Abbé J. Dubois, *Hindu Manners, Customs and Ceremonies*, ed. and trans. H. K. Rupa Beuchamp, (Calcutta: 1992). The arrogant and contemptuous attitude with foreign cultures are considered, i.e. the Hindu as well as the Muslims in India in the case of the European writers of the seventeenth, eighteenth and nineteenth centuries, as uncouth and uncivilised beings, bears an astonishing similarity to the comments that the European writers made on the Ottomans, even in someone like Donà's book, who repeatedly claims the Turks to be generally not intelligent and not in possession of the arts and letters. On this subject, see in addition to Dubois, *also* the travels of Pietro della Valle: Pietro della Valle, *Viaggi di Pietro della Valle, Il Pellegrino, Parte Prima: Turchia, Parte Seconda: Persia, Parte Terza: India*, (Roma: 1662) and François Bernier, *Travels in the Mogul Empire (1656-1668)*, (New Delhi: S. Chand, 1972).

Referring to the European travellers in India, the renowned Indian psychoanalyst Sudhir Kakar says: 'The ethnographers of the seventeenth, eighteenth and nineteenth centuries, who were also the cultural psychologists of their eras, are pre-eminently the European travellers... Lacking any knowledge of the country's religious traditions, the travellers' interest is excited by what appears to them as strange Hindu ceremonies, rituals, and customs – with an emphasis on temple courtesans, burning of widows, and orgiastic religiosity.' See Sudhir Kakar, *The Colors of Violence. Cultural Identities, Religion, and Conflict* (London: The University of Chicago Press, 1996), p. 18.

> Before entering into the study of Turkish Literature, I should remove a great popular error, still rooted in the minds of many erudite Europeans, who firmly feel and write about Muhammad, that he closed every way of science with severe precept, fearing that harm would [come] to his doctrine if sciences were cultivated; making ignorance of his people almost the base upon which to found the extravagant Muslim religion. However, Muhammad was equally concerned, as it would become clear from his own words, of the false prophet: 'It is legitimate', he says, 'for the Muslims to possess all the sciences.' And in another saying of his [he says]: 'Seek science, even if it were in China.' The sentence written on the library of the conqueror of Constantinople is famous: 'The study of sciences is a divine precept for the real believers.' Therefore, it is clearly seen, how far from the truth it is to think that Muhammad wanted to prohibit his people from science and keep them buried in ignorance... The intelligence and happy climate of the Turks, especially the abundance of the Arabic books, the translations of the Greeks, original and perfect masters of all knowledge, honour and solemn advantages, give the Ottomans the fruits of letters.[108]

Strikingly enough, many of the models, prejudices and stereotypes held by the Europeans against the Ottomans in the Age of Enlightenment, viewing the Empire of the Turks as decadent and 'despotic', are still being applied today to other countries in the Middle East. This Enlightenment image of the Turk as 'feminine', 'despotic' and 'somewhat more primitive than us' has been extended to peoples not only in Middle East, but also as far afield as South Asia and India. A book published by the Italian traveller Pietro della Valle entitled *Viaggi di Pietro della Valle, Il Pellegrino*[109] contains his account of his sojourn in India, passing through the Ottoman Empire and Iran. This work is not only an important document relating to the history of these three countries, but also sets up the stereotypical image of the *Orient* which will be found in the coming centuries. As the renowned Indian historian Romila Thapar states, the model of *oriental despotism* viewed the oriental states as static, devoid of evolution and despotic. In a way, the European imagination produced a wholesale image of the Orient. As follows from what has already been said, the images of the Greco-Persian antagonism, the Turks and India are juxtaposed by Thapar:

---

[108] Giambattista Toderini, *Letteratura Turchesca* (Venezia: Presso Giacomo Storti, 1787), pp. 1-3.
[109] Pietro Della Valle, *Viaggi di Pietro della Valle, Il Pellegrino*, Parte I: Turchia, Parte II: Persia, Parte III: India (Roma: Apresso Iacomo Dragondelli, 1662).

> Central to this view of the pre-modern history of India, and implicit in Mill's History, was the theory of oriental despotism. (R. Koebner, 'Despot and despotism: Vicissitudes of a political term', *Journal of the Warburg and Courtauld Institutes*, 1951, 14, pp. 275-80; F. Venturini, 'Oriental Despotism', *Journal of the History of Ideas*, 1963, 24, pp. 133-142.) The genesis of this theory probably goes back to the Greco-Persian antagonism, with references in Greek writing to the despotic government of the Persians. To this was added the vision of the luxuries of the oriental courts, a vision built partly on the luxury trade with the east from early times, and partly on the fantasy world of oriental courts described in the accounts of visitors to these regions, such as those of Ktesias at the Persian court and Megasthenes at the Mauryan court of India. The Crusades and the ensuing literature on the Turks doubtless strengthened the notion of the all-powerful, despotic, oriental potentate.[110]

The image-formation process which placed the Turks in the role of standard-bearers of the alien Islamic culture after the fifteenth century has evolved in our day back into making the Arabs, and this time also the Asiatic Muslims, once again the focal point of the main 'other'. This shift in target of the perceived 'other' to the Middle East and the Asiatic Muslims, especially after the post-colonial age, was partially due to the collapse of the Ottoman Empire and the new orientation of the new Turkish Republic as a secular state. This, however, by no means implies that the past image and the role of the Turks as the 'other' has vanished, as it is clearly seen in the official European political rhetoric vis-à-vis the Turks, transformed onto the European Union platform in the last decades.

One hopes that when the role and a thorough academic study of all aspects of cultural otherness in the East-West relations are further studied, one will get hold of a more objective sense of reality. Whatever the aim of such a study be, the crucial place and the role that the Turks have played in representing the 'other' vis-à-vis Europe seems only to be a fragment, although an important and an indispensable part, of a larger picture of 'otherness' in East-West relations. In this respect, the uniting thread of comparative image studies between the Western perceptions of various Eastern cultures, still remains virgin territory.

---

[110] Romila Thapar, 'Ideology and the Interpretation of Early Indian History', in *Interpreting Early India* (Delhi: Oxford University Press, 1992), p. 6.

# When the Turks saved the Greek Cypriots

## Selective Memories of 300 years under Ottoman Rule

Jan-Erik Smilden

The political question of Cyprus is nearly as inflamed as the conflict between the Israelis and the Palestinians. The Greek Cypriots and the Turkish Cypriots[1] have their separate versions of the island's history, and their narratives are often totally contradictory. But when it comes down to basics, there are sometimes not such great differences between the two versions, it is rather a question of how the history is presented.

The question is also who has won the propaganda war. That is definitely not the Turks or the Turkish Cypriots. Over the centuries, Greeks, Greek Cypriots and pro-Hellenic historians and authors have been in the majority and have also had an important impact on the forming of opinions in Europe. And in recent times, after the Turkish invasion of Cyprus in 1974, we have often seen an amateurish, clumsy, arrogant and perplexed attitude from the varying governments in Ankara, frequently amounting almost to naivety.

The history of Turkish oppression and atrocities in Cyprus is well known, due to the prevailing pro-Greek attitudes. Many of these accounts are true, but there is another side of the coin, which to a great extent has been suppressed in both Greek and other European historical literature. My intention is not to defend the Turks, but to try to balance the picture. For some people, the title of my presentation might be provocative. But I can very well support it, based on varying sources. Actually I will

---

[1] I am fully aware that there were no conceptions of 'Greek Cypriots' or 'Turkish Cypriots' during the Ottoman rule in Cyprus. The population was traditionally described as 'Christian' or 'Muslims'. However, I have, in this paper chosen to use 'Greek Cypriots' and 'Turkish Cypriots' because those are the terms used today.

suggest that Cyprus might have been a Catholic island, like Malta today, had the Turkish invasion not occurred in 1570.

## The Turks are coming

Let us go back to the early summer of the dramatic year of 1570. The Venetians had occupied Cyprus since 1489 and continued the Latinisation of the island, begun by Richard the Lionheart[2], the Templar Knights and later the Frankish kingdom of the Lusignans. The Greek Orthodox Church, which obtained its religious independence from the mother church in Constantinople as early as 488, was in ruins. There was no archbishop, and the four remaining bishops had since Frankish time been confined to the island's rural areas. Many Orthodox churches and monasteries, along with their estates, had been confiscated. Some of the churches, first of all in the towns, were converted to Latin houses of God. In the villages the priests were living in utmost poverty. So what happened when the Turks first captured the capital Nicosia in 1570 and the coastal fortress town of Famagusta the following year?[3]

It was the Venetians who were the enemies of the Turks, not the local Greek Cypriot population. Therefore it was the Latin church that now suffered, and not the Greek Orthodox. From being the Christian underdog in Cyprus, the Orthodox Church gradually achieved a power and wealth it still possesses today. While Latin churches were abolished and Latin priests expelled, the Orthodox archbishop was restored to all the rights he had been deprived of by the Franks and the Venetians. The orthodox bishops returned to the towns and villages they had previously been forced to leave by the Frankish kings. The church regained some of its properties and was able to buy back others, including monasteries. The clergy was also allowed to collect taxes. As I shall explain later, this became very important for the church. And even more important was the power of the archbishop. As the first Orthodox archbishop of Cyprus since the fall of Byzantium he was allowed nearly imperial privileges; to hold a sceptre, wear the purple, and sign his name in red ink.[4] He was an ethnarch, both a political and religious leader of the Greek Cypriots, with a power base that later enabled the late Archbishop Makarios to become president and natural leader of his people in the 1960s. Let us hear what Barbara Lyssarides, the wife of the former Greek Cypriot socialist leader Vassos Lyssarides, writes:

---

[2] Conquered Cyprus in 1191.
[3] It would have been more proper to use the term 'Ottoman', but since most of the sources refer to 'Turks', I will mainly do the same.
[4] Rebecca Bryant, *Imagining the Modern, The Cultures of Nationalism in Cyprus* (London: I.B Tauris, 2004), p. 79.

The archbishop of Cyprus was so powerful by the end of the 18th century that both Greeks and Turks here regarded him as the real governor of the Ottoman-held island rather than the appointed muhassıl[5], some historians claim.[6]

## Venetian Hardship

For the common Cypriot, the Frankish and Venetian rule, with a European-style feudalism, was generally full of hardships. Even if some of the serfs were able to buy their freedom, the taxes and the obligations to the rulers were harsh. The traveller Martin von Baumgarten, who visited Cyprus in the sixteenth century wrote:

> All the inhabitants of Cyprus are slaves to the Venetians, being obliged to pay to the state a third of all their income, whether the product of their ground or corn, wine, oil or of their cattle, or any other thing. Besides every one of them is bound to work for the State two days of the week wherever they shall please to appoint him; and if any shall fail, by reason of some other business of their own, or for indisposition of body, then they are made to pay a fine for as many days as they are absent from their work. And what is more, there is yearly some tax or other imposed on them, with which the poor common people are so flayed and pillaged, that they hardly have wherewithal to keep soul and body together.[7]

Under the Venetians a master could sell a serf whenever he pleased, and the local population was treated as the personal property of their masters. When the Turks came, serfdom was abolished. The former serfs were given freedom and were allowed to own property and transfer ownership to others by way of inheritance, gifts or sale.

What was the Greek Cypriot attitude to the Turkish invasion? The sources are naturally contradictory, but there are certain indications. In the village of Lefkara the local population was punished for not having resisted the Muslim invasion forces in 1570.[8] In general there were few Greek Cypriots who fought for the Venetian cause,

---

[5] A *muhassıl* was a commissioner, the representative in Cyprus of the Grand Vizier or the Sublime Porte.
[6] Barbara Cornwall Lyssarides, *My old Acquaintance, Yesterday In Cyprus* (Nicosia: Kailas Printers & Lithographers LTD, 1999), p. 175.
[7] Claude D. Cobham, *Excerpta Cypria* (1908), p. 55, quoted in Katia Hadjidemetriou, *A History of Cyprus* (Nicosia: Hermes Media Press Ltd, 2002), p. 251.
[8] Ahmet C. Gazioğlu, *The Turks in Cyprus, A Province of the Ottoman Empire (1571-1878)* (London: Rustem & Brother, 1990), p. 32.

except in the two large towns of Nicosia and Famagusta. There are also reports of Greek Cypriots who travelled to the Ottoman capital Istanbul to ask for Turkish help against the Venetians before 1570. In 1569 a delegation of Cypriot serfs petitioned the Grand Vizir Mehmet Sokolli for Turkey to occupy Cyprus.[9]

## 'The Turkish Yoke'

In Greek-Cypriot history the period under Turkish rule from 1571 to 1878 is presented as 'The three hundred dark years'. The people suffered daily under 'the Turkish yoke'. Head words are the forced migration of settlers from Anatolia in today's Turkey, forced Turkification, the extreme burden of taxation, atrocities against Greek Cypriots and the Orthodox Church, misrule by brutal, incompetent and corrupt Turkish leaders and massacres and mass flights from the island.

The Turkish rule in Cyprus was of course not based on liberal, democratic or humanistic principles as we know them today. Regimes were oppressive and brutal, whether they were Ottoman, European or Asian. There is no doubt about Turkish abuses in Cyprus, but one might ask how the situation was experienced and felt by the people at that time. When it comes to the present anti-Turkish attitude among Greek Cypriots, it is relevant to ask the following question: how much of this attitude is caused by general conceptions and misconceptions, nationalistic folklore or/and selective memory? Notwithstanding, there is no doubt that the Turkish invasion of Cyprus in 1974 revived the negative attitude towards the former Ottoman masters of the island.

Some 35,000 Turkish soldiers have occupied the northern part of Cyprus since 1974. After 1571 the sultan in Istanbul kept around 4,000 soldiers in Cyprus, often badly armed. The figure seems to be more or less constant during the Turkish rule. In the 1820s the force was reinforced because of the Greek revolution, but it is interesting to note that the total number was reduced to 840 in the years 1841-1842.[10]

## The Settlers from Anatolia

One of the most controversial aspects of Greek Cypriot history concerns the settlers who came from Anatolia to Cyprus in the years after 1571. Together with Christian converts and the descendants of Turkish soldiers and officers, they constitute today most of the Turkish Cypriot population of the divided island. Because of expulsions of Catholics, war, misrule, natural disasters and diseases, there was a lot of empty

---

[9] Hadjidemetriou, pp. 257 ff.
[10] Gazioğlu, p. 261.

land for agriculture in Cyprus after the Turkish occupation. By a decree in 1572 the Governor encouraged the people who had fled the island to return, with the promise that all their rights would be given back to them. Very few seem to have taken the opportunity, but there are some reports, among them an account of 35 Christian families who came back from exile in Venice to Cyprus, reportedly provided with all the facilities they required.[11] What would have happened if more people had returned, is difficult to say, but the fact is that an 'exile proclamation' was issued on 19th August 1572. One in ten households in four different Turkish provinces in Anatolia were to be transferred to Cyprus to resettle there, voluntarily or by force. The ones who registered but did not leave were to be hanged, something that shows that this policy was not to be lenient. But one important question is whether this was a planned deliberate step to Turkify and Islamise Cyprus, as many Greek Cypriots claim.

According to estimates, 8,000 families from mainland Turkey were resettled in Cyprus by the end of the sixteenth century. Dr. Recep Dündar at İnönü University in Ankara has made an interesting study of who the settlers were. By checking the lists of settlers, he has found out that there were Christian families among them, mostly Greeks, living in Anatolia. Dündar has not found any indication whether the exiles were Muslims or non-Muslims.[12] But the majority living in these areas were Turks, and the majority who arrived in Cyprus were naturally Turks, too. One may speak of a Turkification, but not necessarily a quite deliberate one. As in other parts of the Ottoman empire, the Turkish rulers were mainly interested not in converting the Christian population, but in securing the tax incomes. One can therefore not talk about an Islamisation.

## Burden of Taxation

As in other provinces of the Ottoman Empire, the millet system was established after 1571, with internal self-rule for the different religious communities. The *rayahs*, as the Christians were called, had to pay special taxes for exemption of military service and to practise their own religion. Imperial decrees from the sultan in Istanbul stated that the taxes should be lower than under the Venetians. The tithe was to be between one fifth and one eighth. In practice it seemed more often to be one fifth than one eighth. And even if serfdom was abolished, some feudal practices from the previous era were retained and applied during Turkish rule. In many parts of the island the peasants were obliged to work on state properties one day a week, but it does not seem to have been

---

[11] *Great Ottoman-Turkish Civilisation*, Volum I (Ankara: Yeni Turkiye), p. 261.
[12] Op.cit, pp. 259-274.

a regular practice. There were different taxes, many of them heavy. Even if the order from the sultan in Istanbul was to keep the taxes lower than under the Venetians, there was a lot of over-taxation, based on greed, corruption and tax systems like tax-farming, where a person could buy the rights to collect taxes in a certain area. The Greek Cypriots seem to be mostly correct when focusing on the burden of taxes during the Ottoman rule, but that was not special to Cyprus. There, as in other regions of the world, the oppressed people had a lot of clever and sophisticated ways of evading or reducing taxes, for instance by concealing the real number of animals owned.

Beyond doubt, the peasants were oppressed, but who were the oppressors? The Turks of course, but the Greek-Cypriot historian Katia Hadjidemetriou emphasises that the poor villagers also suffered oppression at the hands of rich Greek landowners. They managed to evade the payment of taxes so that they might be paid by the poor instead.[13] And even more important was the role the Church played in collecting taxes. That right was given to the Orthodox Church after 1571 and extended in 1660. As both parties benefited from the tax incomes, it is also natural that the Turkish leaders and the Orthodox Church often had a close cooperation and a common interest in defending their rights. Here is what the Englishman John Macdonald Kinnair, a captain in the East India Company, wrote after his stay in Cyprus in 1814:

> [T]he Greek peasantry, who are the only industrious class, have been so much oppressed by Turks, monks and bishops, that they are now reduced to the extremity of indigence...[14]

There is no doubt that the Church used some of its income to benefit the Greek-Cypriot people, but it is also a fact that the same Church gathered an abundance of wealth, which even today makes the Greek Cypriot clergy a very influential player in Greek-Cypriot society and politics. One will find little criticism of the Orthodox taxation measures among Greek Cypriots, even if it also meant hardship for the population. In the Greek-Cypriot mind, it is thanks to the Church that they survived as a people and were able to keep their Greekness. This attitude is of course very understandable. But it is also a fact that the Greek Cypriots owe the Turks a great deal because of the power the sultan and the Porte in Istanbul gave the Orthodox Church.

---

[13] Hadjidemetriou, p. 322.
[14] Paul W. Wallace and Andreas G. Orphanides (eds.), *Sources for the History of Cyprus, Volume V, English Texts: Frankish and Turkish Periods* (Altamont New York: Greece and Cyprus Research Center, 1998), p. 148.

# The Power of the Archbishop

The archbishop was not only the political and religious leader of the Greek-Cypriot community, he had also a lot of power in relation to the Turkish governor. He had the right to make complaints to the rulers in Istanbul, and it is established that the archbishop or his envoys travelled to Constantinople many times and presented complaints from the *rayahs* to the Grand Vizier, effectively the Ottoman Prime Minister. Sometimes their missions succeeded, sometimes not. With the declining power of the Ottoman Empire, the archbishop's position in Cyprus increased. The British historian Sir Harry Luke has the following conclusion:

> By an astonishing reversal of fortune the Archbishop of Cyprus, whose office had been created by the Turks after lying dormant for three hundred years, secured in the course of the seventeenth and eighteenth centuries the supreme power and authority over the island and at one period wielded influence greater than that of the Turkish Pasha himself.[15]

There were Turkish abuses against the Orthodox clergy, but in general there was cooperation between the two axes of power. The relationship was, however, seriously harmed by the Greek revolution, starting in Greece in 1821. Some envoys of the Greek nationalist movement, *Philike Hetaireia*, came to Cyprus and tried to convince the Cypriot leaders to rise against their Turkish masters. The archbishop himself became a member of *Philike Hetaireia*. Some Greek Cypriots travelled to Greece to fight against the Turkish enemy. Others collected money in Cyprus to finance the war on the Greek mainland. There were plans and talk about uprisings, and when the Turkish authorities in Cyprus discovered leaflets proclaiming revolution, they reacted. At first the sultan in Istanbul refused to allow any executions, and demanded instead disarmament of the Greek Cypriot population. But the Governor of Cyprus, Küçük Mehmet, at last secured the sultan's permission to execute 486 Cypriots. Among the ones that were executed on the dramatic day of 9th July 1821 were the archbishop, three bishops, several other clergymen and some laymen. More executions followed. Some Cypriots escaped death by fleeing abroad. These executions of course had (and still have) a serious impact on the Greek-Cypriot people who understandably consider the victims as martyrs. But as Greek-Cypriot historians also admit, the Cypriot leaders knew very well that an uprising in Cyprus would have no other consequence than slaughter.[16]

---

[15] Sir Harry Luke, *Cyprus under the Turks 1571-1878* (London: C. Hurst & Company, 1969), p. 17.
[16] Hadjidemetriou, p. 299.

How lasting was the Turkish revenge after 1821, and was the Orthodox Church crushed once and for all? Definitely not. Four thousand Ottoman soldiers, mostly Arabs and Albanians, were sent from Syria to Cyprus as reinforcements to restore order. They behaved very badly and plundered and pillaged Orthodox churches and monasteries. As a consequence the sultan issued a firman, a decree, by which much of the confiscated gold and silver plate of the monasteries and churches was not sold, but returned to Joachim, the new archbishop.[17]

During the Ottoman reform period, the *Tanzimat* in the late 1830s, the power of the Orthodox Church was restored and even strengthened. Also the common Greek Cypriots benefited from these reforms. It is, however, interesting to observe that such reform periods were often opposed by the local Turkish rulers, the Greek upper class and even the Church, who saw their interests threatened by political and economical changes.

## Enosist Aspirations

Three Cypriot uprisings occurred at the beginning of the 1830s, motivated by maladministration and unjust taxes. Two of them, however, also had enosist aspirations, with the aim of uniting Cyprus with Greece.[18] This time the pro-Greek upheavals were not supported by the Orthodox Church. Despite the pro-Greek sentiments of the Greek-Cypriot population, students were allowed to leave Cyprus for studies in Greece, first and foremost in Athens. There they came under the influence of Greek nationalists, and brought aspirations for freedom with them when they came back to Cyprus. The Turkish rulers for one reason or another allowed this to go on. Even more surprising is the fact that in 1846 Greece was allowed to open a Greek consulate in Larnaca to protect the Greek citizens in Cyprus. Some of these Greeks were actually Greek Cypriots who had obtained Greek citizenship after fighting in Greece against the Turks during the Greek war of independence.

The Turks did not care about the *rayahs'* education in Cyprus. When schools were established in the second part of the eighteenth century, this was mainly the responsibility of the Orthodox Church, including financially. Schools and teachers' salaries were financed by taxes imposed by the Church. The curriculum was based on Orthodoxy, Greek language and history. Especially after the Greek revolution, the schools promoted nationalism, more or less without Turkish interference. The Greek-Cypriot pupils did not learn Turkish, neither did the great majority of the Greek

---

[17] Gazioğlu, p. 278.
[18] Stavros Panteli, *The Making of Modern Cyprus. From obscurity to statehood* (Nicosia: Interworld Publications, 1990), pp. 58f.

Cypriot population. It was more common that Turks and Turkish Cypriots learned Greek, and that brings me to another interesting observation. In how many parts of the world did the occupier learn the occupied subjects' language and not vice versa?

Reading Greek-Cypriot history is a constant procession of drought, crop failures, earthquakes, flooding, locust ravages, plagues and fevers. There are few disagreements between Greek-Cypriot and Turkish-Cypriot historians concerning these terrible occurrences, but one can sometimes get the impression that even acts of God are the fault of the Turks in the Greek-Cypriot mind. Population decline was often due to plagues and migration. Migration was sometimes a result of Turkish misrule, at other times a consequence of crop failure due to natural causes. Greek-Cypriot history can tell us that Greek Cypriots often moved to Syria to escape the Turkish yoke in Cyprus. But how can that be possible, when the Turks also ruled Syria for most of this period? It seems to me that one has to look into a lot of different causes for migration and population decline, and to balance the picture.

## Cooperation between the Ethnic Groups

Both Turkish-Cypriot and Greek-Cypriot historians emphasise that the two population groups cooperated during long periods of Ottoman rule. There was no direct affection between them, but they often lived in the same villages, and they were often interacting in daily life. There were few mixed marriages, but the reason was probably more a question of religion than ethnicity. Often the Greek Cypriots and the Turkish Cypriots cooperated in uprisings against the rulers, sometimes these uprisings were a protest against tax burdens imposed both by the Turkish rulers and the Orthodox clergy. The Greek revolution spread some fear among the Turkish Cypriots, but it was not until the 1950s, under British rule, that the ethnic groups started to drift totally apart.

Cyprus was of course no heaven on earth, neither for the Greek Cypriots nor for the Turkish Cypriots. Daily life was often hard, but foreign travellers were often surprised by some positive elements. One factor often mentioned is the absence of criminality. The English vice-consul wrote in 1862 that 'Brigandage, burglaries and assassinations are so rare as to be almost unknown in Cyprus.'[19] His assertion is also confirmed by many other sources. There is no doubt that the Cypriots have been oppressed during their history, but it might perhaps be more relevant and fruitful to speak about 800 years of darkness, from 1191 to 1960, when Cyprus obtained independence from Great Britain. It was actually the British occupation that led

---
[19] Hadjedemitriou, p. 329.

to the most serious and bloody rebellion, orchestrated by the militant organisation EOKA B in the 1950s. As an indication of the 800 years of darkness I shall quote from the writings of the hermit St Neophytos in the district of Paphos in the first years of the thirteenth century, during the Frankish period:

> Strange things and unheard of have befallen this land, and such that all its rich men have forgotten their wealth, their fine dwellings, families, servants, slaves, their many flocks, herds, swine, cattle of all kinds, grainbearing fields, fertile vineyards and variegated gardens, and with great care and secrecy have sailed away to foreign lands, and to the queen of cities. And those who could not fly – who is fit to set forth the tragedy of their sufferings?[20]

## Conclusion

As we have seen the Turks restored the Orthodox Church with its extensive power. But what would have happened if the Turks had not conquered Cyprus in 1571? As always with counterfactual questions, it is difficult to give a clear and certain answer, but it is doubtful if the Orthodox Church would have survived, at least economically. On the local level it might have, in a way, kept its position, but without any income, except from local support. Another question is how long the Latin rulers would have allowed the Orthodox Church to exist at all, due to the bad relations between the two Christian churches. The Venetians would definitely have tried to wipe out Hellenism from Cyprus, had they kept their power. The Orthodox Church and Hellenism was the glue that kept the Greek-Cypriot people together during hundreds of years of occupation. They could have survived until the Greek revolution of 1821 and thereafter been 'liberated' by their Greek brethren. But that is just a mere supposition.

Let me finish my essay with a quotation from the book *British Cyprus* written by the British author and traveller to the island in 1878, William Hepworth Dixon. He characterised the relationship between the Turkish Governor Bessim Pasha and the Orthodox Archbishop Sophronios II in the following way: 'Bessim held the whip, but Geronymo (Sophronios) showed him where to strike.'[21]

---

[20] Claude Cobham, *Excerpta Cypria*, pp. 10-11, quoted in Katia Hadjidemetriou, *A History of Cyprus* (Nicosia: Hermes Media Press Ltd., 2002), p. 173.
[21] Gazioğlu, p. 254.

# Bibliography

Bryant, Rebecca, *Imagining the Modern, The cultures of Nationalism in Cyprus* (London: I.B. Tauris, 2004).

Dündar, Recep, *The Conquest and Settlement of Cyprus, in Great Ottoman-Turkish Civilisation*, Volume I (Ankara: Yeni Turkiye, 2002).

Gazioğlu, Ahmed C., *The Turks In Cyprus. A Province of the Ottoman Empire (1571-1878)* (London: K. Rustem & Brother, 1990).

Hadjidemetriou, Katia, *A History of Cyprus* (Nicosia: Hermes Media Press Ltd, 2002).

Luke, Sir Harry, *Cyprus under the Turks 1571-1878* (London: C Hurst & Company, 1969).

Lyssarides, Barbara Cornwall, *My old Acquaintance, Yesterday in Cyprus* (Nicosia: Kailas Printers and Lithographers LTD, 1999).

Panteli, Stavros, *The Making of Modern Cyprus, From obscurity to statehood* (Nicosia: Interworld Publications, 1990).

Paul W. Wallace and Andreas G. Orphanides, *Sources for the History of Cyprus. Volume V, English Texts: Frankish and Turkish Periods* (Altamont, New York: Greece and Cyprus Research Center, 1998).

# Turkey seen from Europe's 'Near East', the Balkans

Svein Mønnesland

## Introduction

Until the early twentieth century, south-eastern Europe, known since the nineteenth century as the Balkans, was not considered a part of Europe proper. Terms like 'the Near East' and 'the Near Orient' were used, or, later, 'European Turkey' and 'Turkey-in-Europe'. Unlike the rest of Europe, for whom the Ottoman threat was more or less distant, and the Turks represented a distant 'Otherness', the peoples of south-eastern Europe lived for centuries directly under Ottoman rule. Their societies, their way of life, mentality, language and even religious beliefs to some extent, were influenced by the Ottomans. In what does this Ottoman legacy consist, and to what extent is it a reality in the present-day Balkan states? How is this legacy reflected in their attitude towards present-day Turkey? Let us first recapitulate the historical events.

## The Ottoman Expansion

From the middle of the fourteenth century, a Turkic empire under the Ottoman dynasty established itself over the Balkans. At the time of Osman (1299-1326), the founder of the dynasty, the Byzantine Empire was still suffering the consequences of the Crusade of 1202-1204 when Constantinople was destroyed. The Byzantine Empire that was re-established in 1261 was only a shadow of its former strength. In the second half of the fourteenth century the other Balkan states were also weakened, Serbia after Tsar Dusan's death in 1355 and Bulgaria after the last important ruler Ivan Alexander's death in 1371. However, the Ottoman expansion was slow; it took two centuries to conquer the whole Balkan peninsula, including parts of Hungary. The most important events were the battle of Maritsa in 1371 and the fall of Sofia in 1385, the battle of Kosovo in 1389 and the subsequent reduction of Serbia, the fall of

Constantinople in 1453, the fall of Belgrade in 1459, the fall of the Bosnian kingdom in 1463, the battle of Mohács in 1526, and the siege of Vienna in 1529. Only fringe areas stayed outside Ottoman rule, Croatia proper (under what was left of Hungary), Dalmatia (under Venice), Dubrovnik/Ragusa (semi-independent, paying tribute to the Ottomans) and part of Montenegro. The Habsburg Empire was to become Europe's bulwark against the Turks.

In these fringe areas, just outside the Ottoman Empire, Turkish expansion was a constant threat. No wonder that the national epic poems of these nations all glorified the fight against the Turks: in seventeenth century Dubrovnik there was *Osman* by Ivan Gundulić, in nineteenth century Croatia *Smail Aga's Death* by Ivan Mažuranić and in Montenegro *The Mountain Wreath* by Petar Petrović Njegoš. Among the Christian populations living under Ottoman rule, no such epic works could be written, but here flourished epic folk songs, glorifying the struggle against the Turks. The Battle of Kosovo was remembered in song as a crucial event for the Serbian nation, and the legendary hero Prince Marko accomplished heroic, supernatural deeds against the Turks. The *haiduks*, outlaws plundering the Turks in the mountainous regions of the Balkans, became heroes. This folk epic clearly had the function of maintaining moral resistance to foreign rule. The Orthodox Church used this tradition in order to keep alive the memories of the Serbian medieval state and the glory of the Church. This heroic epic tradition was to dominate Serbian culture and the Serbian mentality until the present time.

The urban centres in the Balkans were completely orientalised. This oriental urban culture, with its bazaars and artisans, had an enormous impact on Balkan culture and the Balkan mentality. Even today the word *čaršija*, meaning oriental bazaar, is used in Serbian to denote the political life of the capital. In Sarajevo the Turkish bazaar, the *Baščaršija*, still exists. The peoples of the Balkans, Slavs, Albanians, Greeks and Romanians alike, were deeply influenced by the centuries under Ottoman rule. Their food, folk music and language came under Turkish influence. Today the 'national' dishes of these different Balkan nations are mostly similar, with Turkish names adapted to the different languages. The collection of articles in *Die Türkei in Europa* (Grothusen 1979) presents studies on Turkish influence in Europe in the fields of history, art, language, religion and economy.

However, only in Bosnia and among Albanians did an extensive conversion to Islam take place. The bulk of the Balkan population continued to be Orthodox Christians, enjoying religious freedom, thanks to the relatively tolerant attitude of the Ottomans towards religion. The Empire was administered according to religious groups, the so-called millet system, organised in Christian (Orthodox), Jewish and Armenian millets. The Greek Orthodox Patriarch was a high-ranking official in

Istanbul, responsible for tax-collection among his fellow believers. An account of the coexistence of Muslims and Christians in the Balkans, with rich pictorial material, is given in *Muslim und Christen. Das Osmanische Reich in Europa*, by Hegyi and Ziumányi (1986). The religious tolerance of the Ottomans does not mean, however, that there was no discrimination. The non-Muslim population did not enjoy the same rights as the true believers. This might be one reason for the conversion to Islam, especially in Bosnia, which seems to have taken place without coercion (see Pinson 1993 for a survey of the history of the Bosnian Muslims).

## The Ottoman Retreat

By the end of the seventeenth century, after the second siege of Vienna in 1683, the Ottoman Empire began a slow but steady contraction. In the Ottoman possessions in the Balkans, revolutionary national movements began with the first Serbian uprising in 1804, which led to the creation of a semi-independent Principality of Serbia in 1830. Greece also won its independence in 1830. Montenegro was de facto independent from Ottoman rule after 1796. Bosnia was ruled by a native Slav Muslim nobility, unwilling to modernise, even rising in armed rebellion against Ottoman authority. This led to a series of uprisings among the mainly Christian Orthodox peasantry. In 1875 the uprising spread throughout Bosnia and Herzegovina, which gave Serbia, Montenegro and Russia an opportunity for war against Turkey and the European powers the opportunity for intervention. The Treaty of San Stefano ended the Russian-Turkish war with a Russian victory. Since the Western powers could not tolerate Russian domination in the Balkans, the Treaty of Berlin (1878) settled the borders, and let Austria-Hungary occupy Bosnia-Herzegovina, which made many Bosnian Muslims emigrate to Ottoman territory. After a while, however, the Bosnian Muslims became quite satisfied with Austrian rule, while the Serbs became the main opponents to Austrian rule in Bosnia. For Serbia, both Austria-Hungary and the Ottoman Empire represented obstacles to achieving a Great Serbian state, including all or most of the Serbs in the region. For an account of the 'Balkanisation' of the Balkans, the rise of independent states, see Jelavich (1977) and Barbara Jelavich (1983).

'The Eastern Question', the issue of the future of Turkish possessions in the Balkans, became a major preoccupation of the great powers towards the end of the nineteenth century and the beginning of the twentieth. In the first Balkan War of 1912, the Christian Balkan states solved the problem by the expulsion of the Turks from Europe, except the area around Istanbul and the city itself (which is still Turkey-in-Europe). Unable to divide the occupied territories peacefully, the Second

Balkan War (1913) ended with a Bulgarian defeat, with Serbia and Greece dividing Macedonia, while the Western powers established an Albanian state.

## Anti-Turkish Nationalism

The new Balkan states that emerged during the nineteenth century were conceived as nation states. Nationalism, imported through the German tradition, was based on the notion of a common language, history, culture and religion. The cornerstone of nation-building was the liberation of Christian peasants from their Turkish overlords, and the struggle of the Orthodox churches against Islam. The Turkish rule was depicted in black colours. The demonisation of the Turks and celebration of the pre-Ottoman states was the very foundation of the new states. Symptomatic was the title of the 1889 novel by Bulgaria's national writer Ivan Vazov, *Under the Yoke* [*Pod igoto*].

In the new national states the mixed nature of the populations presented a problem. Minorities, and especially Muslim ones, had no place in the newborn states. From the very beginning of the Balkanisation process, i.e. the emergence of new states, there was a steady flow of Muslim refugees, especially Turks, to areas still held by the Ottomans. This was in part a forced migration, often resembling ethnic cleansing. The slogan was, at least implicitly, Greece for the Greeks, Serbia for the Serbs etc. Although demonising the Turks, the different Balkan nations, Slavs, Greeks, Rumanians and Albanians, continued to be deeply influenced by the Ottoman legacy in their way of life, mentality, food, music and language (oriental loanwords). Even today this legacy is what distinguishes the Balkan cultures from Central or Western European culture. Although the anti-Turkish attitude is strong in Serbia, much of their popular music (the so-called *turbo folk*) is of oriental inspiration, a tendency that has even grown more prominent during the last decades, despite the official hostility to anything Turkish and Oriental.

## Different Views of the Ottoman Empire

The negative picture of the Ottoman Empire ('The Turkish yoke') has been the prevailing one in Balkan discourse, and it has also been reinforced by scholarly works. An example is the 1924 doctoral dissertation of the Nobel prize winner Ivo Andrić, *The Development of Spiritual Life in Bosnia under the Influence of Turkish Rule* (written in German, at the University of Graz). Andrić's view was clearly anti-Turkish. He found no cultural values in the oriental tradition in Bosnia:

> All researchers into Bosnia and its past, be they Serbo-Croatian or foreign, have felt in a position to state in concert and more or less forcefully that the effect of Turkish rule was absolutely negative. ... The Turks could bring no cultural content or sense of higher historic mission, even to those South Slavs who accepted Islam; for their Christian subjects, their hegemony brutalised custom and meant a step to the rear in every respect.[1]

Today one can find quite opposing views on the Ottoman Empire. Some reflect the traditional hostile attitude among the Christian population in the Balkans, others a more moderate view, or even an extremely positive one. An example of the traditional concept of the Ottoman Empire would be the following, taken from a 1980 history of Albanian literature:

> These five centuries of foreign occupation were a period of tremendous hardships in the history of the Albanian people. The destruction of urban centres, the devastation of flourishing districts by the repeated expeditions and incursions of the invaders, and the decimation of the population, turned the country into a deplorable situation. Economic and social development came to a standstill and the country was flung some centuries backward.[2]

On the other hand, a positive view was put forward in January 2005 by the influential Bosnian Muslim Adil Zulfikarpašić, founder and director of the Bosniak Institute in Zürich and Sarajevo:

> More and more is brought to light the enormous civilizing and cultural role of Turkey, halting the feudal Europeans, who greedy for territories and wealth, wanted to subjugate Asia and Africa. And Turkey brought a higher level of civilisation, and higher standard and quality of life, than existed before they came.[3]

However, this positive view does not necessarily reflect a common view among Bosnian Muslims. The leading circles in the Islamic community in Bosnia are not oriented towards Turkey, which they find too secularised. They look to Iran, Egypt and other Islamic countries for spiritual education and inspiration. Although it is commonly believed that the Bosnian Muslims represent a modern, European form

---

[1] Andrić, 1990, p. 38.
[2] Bihiku, p. 6.
[3] Zulfikarpašić, p. 14.

of Islam, the Atatürk legacy in Turkey prevents them from using modern Turkey as a model for Bosnia.

If we turn to the extreme nationalist discourse, the traditional concept of struggle between Christianity and Islam is kept alive, especially among nationalist Serbs. In the Bosnian war of 1992-1995, the Serb nationalists commonly used the term 'Turks' to refer to the Bosnian Muslims, thereby connecting the present war with the centuries old struggle against the Ottoman Turks. The Serb leader Radovan Karadžić even raised the threat of a possible revival of the Ottoman Empire:

> We Serbs have been under the Turks for a long time, so we know what they want. They want to return to Europe as a great power, as a great empire, such as they once were. Also the Bulgarians and Greeks are menaced together with us, and they fully understand us. The Serbs for sure will not tolerate Turkey's return to Serbian territories. The Turks are mistaken in their undertakings, because history once happens as tragedy, the second time being repeated as farce. So, the Turks' attempt to return to Europe as a great power is a farce and the Serbs will defend their territory.[4]

In this rhetorical discourse, the Christian Balkan nations are seen as a bulwark against the Oriental East, as Europe's outpost against the Muslim threat.

## The Balkans' 'in-betweenness'

Seen from Western Europe, the Balkans was half Oriental. The term 'Balkan' acquired a pejorative meaning, as opposed to the allegedly higher European civilisation. In *Imagining the Balkans*, Maria Todorova (1997), following Said's analysis of Orientalism, tries to explain 'how could a geographical appellation /the Balkans/ be transformed into one of the most powerful pejorative designations in history, international science and nowadays, general intellectual discourse?' Todorova draws attention to the Balkans' 'transitory character, their "in-betweeness".'[5] According to Todorova, the negative picture of the Balkans is due to the West's concept of the Ottoman legacy. The strong impact that the Ottoman past had in the Balkans was interpreted as totally negative, and an artificial concept of the Balkans as half Turkish was created in the West.

---

[4] Karadžić, p. 21, my translation.
[5] Todorova, p. 7.

However, this negative concept is also found in the Balkans. The old border between the Habsburg and Ottoman Empires still divides the peninsula. Seen from the Western part of the Balkan Peninsula, Croatia, including Dalmatia, it is only the Eastern part of the peninsula that is marked by its Ottoman legacy. Croatia was traditionally called the *Antemurale Christianitatis*, Europe's bulwark against the Muslims (and the Orthodox). But, as we have seen, Orthodox Christians in the Balkans may use the same rhetoric of being Europe's outpost against the Orient. This different aspects of the border between 'we – Europeans' and 'they – Orientals' has been called 'nesting Balkanisms' (Bakic-Hayden 1995). The negative picture of the Oriental legacy has deeply influenced the Balkan peoples themselves.

## Present-day Relations with Turkey

Presently the Balkan states are rapidly improving their relationship with Turkey. The common goal of EU membership is the main reason. Very little is, apparently, left of the old antagonism, at least on a state level. On April 1st 2005 a Council of the Ministers of Culture of South Eastern Europe was founded, consisting of Albania, Bulgaria, Greece, Croatia, Macedonia, Romania, Turkey and Serbia-Montenegro, whose aim is to intensify cultural cooperation in the region. In September 2004 Serbia-Montenegro and Turkey signed an agreement on military cooperation, Serbia-Montenegro's first agreement with a NATO country. Prime Minister Tadić said: 'Relations between Serbia and Turkey are a prerequisite for political stability in the Balkans and we will do everything to improve the relations in the coming years.'[6]

Two states have had a particularly complicated relationship with Turkey: Greece and Bulgaria, the two Balkan countries sharing a common border with Turkey. Tensions between Greece and Turkey go back to the Greek-Turkish war of 1919-1922, which ended with the Treaty of Lausanne. Since the Second World War, Greece's dispute with Turkey over territorial rights and interests in the Aegean Sea and especially over Cyprus since the Turkish invasion in 1974, is well known. The two NATO countries were on the brink of war in 1986 and 1987. Deeply rooted historical antagonism is the hallmark of the Greek-Turkish relationship, mostly due to ethnic questions. After the disintegration of the Ottoman Empire, a considerable Turkish minority remained in Greece, but was diminished through the reciprocal exchange of the Turkish population in Western Thrace with the Greek population in Turkey in the 1920s. In the late 1980s, there were cases of anti-Turk discrimination in Western Thrace, the Greek authorities claiming that the Turks there were in fact

---

[6] Tanjug (Yugoslav News Agency), 20 August 2004.

'Greek Muslims'. For a long time Greece blocked Turkish candidacy for EU membership, the Greeks demanding that Turkish membership depend on its recognition of Cyprus. Turkey was the only state not to recognise the EU-member Cyprus and the only one to recognise the breakaway Turkish Republic of Northern Cyprus. Turkey, on the other hand, maintained that recognition of Cyprus is out of the question.

Bulgaria has also had a complicated relationship with its eastern neighbour. After the fall of the Ottoman Empire, a considerable Turkish minority was left in Bulgaria. Ever since the establishment of an autonomous Bulgarian principality in 1878, there has been an emigration of ethnic Turks from Bulgaria to Turkey, partly spontaneous, partly organised through population transfer agreements, both before and after the Second World War. According to the latest census held in 2001, there are 746,664 ethnic Turks in Bulgaria, or 9.4 per cent of the total population. During the communist regime, a harsh assimilation policy was carried out, the most spectacular aspect being the renaming campaign from the mid-1980s, when Turks were forced to take Slavic names. Since Bulgaria and Turkey, during the Cold War, belonged to opposite blocs, Turkey could not interfere. When communism was falling, in June-August 1989, approximately 350,000 ethnic Turks left Bulgaria for Turkey. Turkey took a critical, but balanced position. With the end of the Cold War and the fall of the Zhivkov regime, a new policy was introduced. In 1994 the Bulgarian government granted the emigrants the right to retain or regain their Bulgarian citizenship. Currently the Turkish ethnic population in Bulgaria enjoys extensive rights. After the elections of 2001, the Turkish political party was included in the government with two ministers. There is an extensive literature on the situation of the Bulgarian Turks, for an overview see the publication by the Bulgarian Helsinki Committee (2003).

Although Turkey has considered itself as a protector of the Turkish diaspora, the policy has been to avoid conflict with Bulgaria. Nor does the significant community of Turkish immigrants from Bulgaria in Turkey, about 700,000, present any problem. On the contrary, it may have contributed to the normalisation process. Today the relations between Bulgaria and Turkey are very good, with no serious political problems. Economic cooperation has developed after the signing of a free trade agreement. The European Union is financing a cross-border cooperation programme. Bulgaria is now the country that Turkey has the best neighbourly relations with.

# Conclusion

Despite the historical legacy of hatred and mistrust, the present-day Balkan states have, during the last few years, developed good relations with Turkey. The exception is Greece, and its unresolved disputes with Turkey. But even Greek-Turkish relations have become more relaxed since Turkish membership of the EU came on the agenda, and there is hope that Turkey will normalise its relations with Greece and Cyprus, in order to start negotiations. Among the other Balkan states, there seems to be no opposition to Turkish EU membership. Moreover, they consider Turkish membership as a benefit for themselves. Romania and Bulgaria joined the EU in 2007 and see advantages in having Turkey as a member, themselves serving as a bridge between Europe and Turkey. For the other Balkan states, Macedonia, Serbia, Montenegro, Bosnia-Herzegovina and Albania, Turkish membership can be seen as support for their own ambitions of European integration. If this picture is accurate, the European Union has managed to help the Balkan countries overcome at least one aspect of centuries old hatred in the region, their deep antagonism towards Turkey.

# Bibliography

Andrić, Ivo, *Die Entwicklung des geistigen Lebens in Bosnien unter der Einwirkung der türkischen Herrschaft* (Graz, 1924).

Andrić, Ivo, *The Development of Spiritual Life in Bosnia under the Influence of Turkish Rule*, edited and translated by Želimir B. Juričić and John F. Loud (Durham and London: Duke University Press, 1990).

Bakic-Hayden, Milica, 'Nesting Orientalisms: The Case of Former Yugoslavia', *Slavic Review*, Vol. 54, No. 4 (1995), pp. 917-931.

Bihiku, Koco, *A History of Albanian Literature* (Tirana, 1980).

Grothusen, Klaus-Detlev (ed.), *Die Türkei in Europa* (Göttingen: Vandenhoeck & Ruprecht, 1979).

Hegui, Klára, Vera Zimányi, *Muslime und Christen. Das Osmanische Reich in Europa* (Budapest: Corvina, 1986).

*The Human Rights of Muslims in Bulgaria in Law and Politics since 1878* (Sofia: Bulgarian Helsinki Committee, 2003).

Hupchick, Dennis P., *The Balkans. From Constantinople to Communism* (New York: Palgrave, 2002).

Jelavich, Barbara, *History of the Balkans. Vol. 1. Eighteenth and Nineteenth Centuries* (Cambridge: Cambridge University Press, 1983).

Jelavich, Charles and Barbara, *The Establishment of the Balkan National States 1804-1920*, A History of East Central Europa Vol. VIII (Seattle and London: University of Washington Press, 1977).

Karadžić, Radovan, 'Intervju', *Pogledi*, Nov. 12 1993.

Pinson, Mark (ed.), *The Muslims of Bosnia-Herzegovina. Their Historic Development from the Middle Ages to the Dissolution of Yugoslavia*, Harvard Middle Eastern Monographs XXVIII, 1993.

Poulton, Hugh and Suha Taji-Farouki (eds.), *Muslim Identity and the Balkan State* (London: Hurst & Company, 1997).

Todorova, Maria, *Imagining the Balkans* (Oxford: Oxford University Press, 1997).

Zulfikarpašić, Adil, 'Intervju', *Feral Tribune*, 2. Jan. 2005.

# The Image of the Turks and Turkey as depicted by Scandinavian Travellers

Bernt Brendemoen

## Introduction

It is no surprise that the Scandinavian travellers who have given the most comprehensive reports on the Turks and the different aspects of the Ottoman Empire have been Swedes. This is quite understandable considering not only the Swedish empire that comprised a considerable part of Eastern Europe from the sixteenth to the beginning of the eighteenth century, but also from the fact that the Swedes and the Ottomans were allied for a long period against the Russians. The Swedish King Charles XII sought refuge in Turkey after his defeat at Poltava in 1709, where he lived under the protection of the Sultan for six years. In fact, because he stayed so long and lived at the expense of the court and did not seem to have any intention of leaving, he acquired the nickname of *Demirbaş*, which means 'piece of inventory'. It was after the return of *Demirbaş* to Sweden in 1715, with an entourage including Turkish servants, that several Turkish words entered the Swedish language such as *kåldolmar* and *kalabalik*, and it was in the time of the same king that it became a custom to give frigates in the Swedish navy Turkish names such as *Yildirim* and *Yaramaz*, meaning 'lightening' and 'ill-behaved' or 'naughty' respectively. After the return of Charles to Sweden, delegations were sent to Istanbul in order to pay off his debts, and it was in connection with one of these official visits that a very spectacular site was purchased where eventually the first permanent Embassy building, Palais de Suède, was erected,[1] and where the Swedish Consulate General and the Swedish Research Institute are situated today.

---

[1] Callmer 1985, p. 48

Bernt Brendemoen

## The Seventeenth Century

Although Charles XII represents the zenith of Swedish-Ottoman relations, there had also been a considerably earlier period of lively diplomatic activity between Sweden and the Ottoman Empire, i.e. during the so-called Thirty Years War. The first Swedish envoy to Istanbul was Paul Strasbourk, who wrote a long report in Latin in 1630 (which remains unpublished). Approximately 30 years later, a most interesting report on Istanbul and the Turkish way of life was written by the Swedish diplomat Claes Brodersson Rålamb (1622-1698), who stayed in Istanbul in 1657/8. His report, published by Christian Callmer in 1963, is remarkable in comparison with most earlier and contemporary descriptions from the point of view of objectivity and lack of bias. While Rålamb was still in Istanbul, the Swedish King sent another envoy there, and in his delegation there were two Germans, the priest Conrad Jacob Hiltebrand and Johann Ulrich von Wallich, who also wrote reports on their stay in Istanbul, and who to some extent describe the same events as Rålamb. If we compare the three, we find that while Rålamb has an open mind and is objective, but at the same time humorous, Hiltebrand describes everything according to his own standards, never concealing his contempt towards the Turks and their religion and culture. For instance, Rålamb, Wallich, and Hiltebrand all visited ceremonies of different kinds of dervishes (which I shall comment on later) and it is very typical of Hiltebrand that he characterises the ceremony as *Gauckeley* (buffoonery), and adds*: 'Mein Recompens Vor diese Curiosität zu sehen war ein guter Kopfstoss und hohngelächter'* (p. 148).[2] In an earlier article, I have made a comparison between these traveller reports and tried to place them within a context of travel literature dealing with Turkey up to the middle of the seventeenth century (Brendemoen 1988a).

The difference between Rålamb and Wallich becomes clear in their treatment of the Turkish religion. Both of them consulted a famous Polish renegade at the Ottoman court, Wojciech Bobowski, alias Albertus Bobovius, alias Ali Ufki, who gave them a treatise about the Muslim religion he had written in Latin. While Rålamb presents this treatise in a Swedish translation as an appendix to his diary, Wallich furnishes it with a lot of subjective comments and observations and notes with reference to earlier travellers. *Närrisch* [foolish] and *lächerlich* [ridiculous] are epithets he uses very frequently. After all, Wallich's chapter on the Muslim religion is meant just to serve as a basis for his subsequent chapters on Antichrist, where he tries to prove that the Muslim and Catholic religions are almost the same thing.

It is not very likely that Rålamb had any deeper understanding of Islam. If he had, he would probably not have given the statement that the *bayram*, the religious feast

---

[2] 'My reward for seeing this strange sight was to be able to throw my head back in derisive laughter.'

which is celebrated for three days when the fast comes to an end, commemorates the fact that Muhammad found the camel he had been searching for for 30 days (p. 129). On the other hand, he never makes any contemptuous remarks about Turkish culture or religion. At the end of the appendix on Islam, however, he adds: 'This kind of madness is what the religion of the Turks consists of' (p. 229), but we may assume that he had to give some statement showing that the extremely positive picture of Islam he had presented had not affected him personally. After all, the diary was kept to be presented to the most Protestant King of Sweden.

Rålamb has not only furnished posterity with a very interesting report, he also brought back with him from Istanbul more than 30 huge paintings, and in particular some depicting processions of dignitaries in Istanbul. These paintings, which are kept at Nordiska Museet in Stockholm, have recently been the subject of a research project undertaken by the Swedish Institute in Istanbul. The result is a magnificent book, *The Sultan's Procession*, edited by Karin Ådahl (Ådahl 2006), which contains eleven articles on the paintings, on Claes Brorson Rålamb, on Istanbul as it was at the time of his visit, and related subjects. Talking of paintings, it should also be mentioned that the Swedish Celsing family, who served as ambassadors to the Ottoman Empire for several generations in the eighteenth century, commissioned paintings depicting Turkish daily life that they brought back with them to Sweden, to their family estate at Biby, near Eskilstuna, where they can still be admired (Ådahl 2003).

Travellers' reports from the Orient and especially from the Ottoman Empire seem to have already become a literary genre in the seventeenth century, and it is obvious that the travellers read each other's reports and copied them to a certain extent. The most important of the earliest reports is the one written by the Flemish diplomat Busbecq, who was an envoy of the Austrian Empire to Istanbul from 1554 to 1562. Quite a number of the subjects treated by him have become *topoi* also used by travellers such as Rålamb, Hiltebrant and Wallich, for example the kindness of the Turks towards birds, their dislike of dogs, which, however, is superseded by love and kindness if the dog happens to be a pregnant bitch or a puppy, in which case they make small shelters for them and put rags under them so that they can lie comfortably. Also the account of the jackals, which enter peoples' houses and steal all kinds of things, but which betray themselves by their howl, which resembles laughter, most probably also originates from Busbecq.

# The Nineteenth Century

If we now make a huge leap towards our time, and land in the 1840s, we find one of the finest and most poetic descriptions of Istanbul ever written. The author is none other than the famous Dane Hans Christian Andersen, who owes most of his reputation to his fairytales. He made a journey to the countries in the Eastern Mediterranean in 1840/1, and published his impressions under the title *En Digters bazar* (Copenhagen 1843/4), which has been published in English at least twice under the title *A Poet's Bazaar*.

Moving approximately sixty years further forward, to 1899, we find another very interesting description written by the Norwegian Knut Hamsun, published in 1905 under the title *Under Halvmånen*, which is a part of the anthology *Stridende liv*. To my knowledge it has never been translated into English, but it was translated into German a year after it appeared in Norwegian. Hamsun visited Istanbul with his first wife, on the way back to Europe from his better known journey to the Caucasus, which he described in *I Æventyrland*, and which can be found in the same anthology.

If we compare Andersen's and Hamsun's works, as well as those of Rålamb and his fellow travellers, we are struck by the fact that there are again certain *topoi* found in all of them due to the fact that there were certain 'musts' for a foreign visitor in Istanbul, or to put it more bluntly, there were certain 'tourist traps' that could or should not be avoided. The fact that these sights and experiences are described in almost all early travel books, and that the descriptions of them tend to be so similar that one may be tempted to postulate a special literary tradition, has become the basis of an interesting field of research thanks to Orhan Pamuk's recent book *Istanbul – Hatıralar ve Şehir*.[3] This is partly an autobiography (up to the age of around 21) and partly a book about Istanbul. It has some very interesting chapters where the author goes through the reports of French travellers from the middle of the nineteenth century, namely Gérard de Nerval, who visited the city in 1842, Théophile Gautier (1852), and Gustave Flaubert (1859). Pamuk's main aim in these chapters is to prove that these authors noticed and described the melancholy of the city in an excellent way, and furthermore that their descriptions of the city in the twentieth century directly inspired Turkish authors such as Ahmet Hamdi Tanpınar and Yahya Kemal in their efforts to create a nationalist picture of Istanbul after the destruction of the Ottoman Empire during the First World War. By the time of these above-mentioned French authors and other European authors of the nineteenth century, the tradition of describing Istanbul that had begun in the sixteenth and seventeenth centuries must have developed into something like a literary genre. This genre or tradition was further developed by the French travellers, and it is very probable that our Scandinavian travellers should be seen as part of this tradition. After all, Istanbul

---

[3] English translation by Maureen Freely erroneously entitled *Istanbul – Memories of a City* (London: Faber and Faber, 2005), Norwegian translation by myself (*Istanbul – byen og minnene*, Oslo: Gyldendal, 2006).

had become a magnet for European travellers, who (e.g. Flaubert) believed that the city would become the capital of the world a hundred years later.[4]

In the case of Hans Christian Andersen, who visited the city before any of these three Frenchmen, the influence must of course have been from other authors, but given that Andersen's book was published in English as early as 1846, it is not impossible that some European travellers may have been influenced by him. However, it should also be kept in mind that while the almost compulsory recurrence of certain *topoi* in all travel books may owe something to literary tradition, it may also be due to the fact that all tourists in Istanbul in former times (much more than is the case today) seem to have been an easy prey of Greek and Armenian guides in particular who spoke a lot of European languages and who of course had their own tradition of what they thought foreign tourists would like to see.[5]

## The Dervishes

One of the most important of the 'musts' for a tourist to Istanbul was a visit to a dervish ceremony. Since the dervish orders were closed down by Atatürk, this is no longer among the main tourist attractions, but because the prohibition has been eased somewhat in recent years (i.e. since Turgut Özal's regime in the 1980s), some of the orders have become more active again. In fact, the very conspicuous and beautiful ceremony of the Mevlevi dervishes, often called 'the Whirling Dervishes' in English, has existed more or less for touristic reasons for many years, but has attracted only those tourists with special interests, as the performances have been very irregular.

But in former times, going to a dervish ceremony seems to have been compulsory, and not only to one, but at least two. Most travellers[6] describe both a visit to the Mevlevi dervishes and the more frightening Rufais or similar more violent orders (known in English as 'the Howling Dervishes'). Andersen's report on the Howling Dervishes is almost like a horror story, and is introduced by a frightening description of a dervish order in Libya related to him by a man he meets on a boat across the Bosphorus. He then relates the ceremony he witnesses in the tiniest detail, for example:

> The dance started, and then a person entered, the most frightening human being I have ever seen. He was a hermit from the district of Medina, my interpreter told me. Never I have seen a human being whose eyes radiated

---
[4] Pamuk 2003, p. 14.
[5] The importance of the guides for the great topical resemblance between the travel books is in fact mentioned by Pamuk, *Istanbul*, p. 224.
[6] E.g. Gautier 1990, pp. 131-148

madness to the same extent as this one… Two young Turks were squatting outside the half circle and conducted the chanting, which continually rose with a monotonous stress. The whole dynasty of Muhammad was gone through from Abdallah to Muhammad, and the choir answered: 'La ilaha ilallah!' In the end it sounded like a damp howl or a snore. Some of them were deathly pale, others the colour of blood, and sweat was pouring down their faces. The hermit threw off his big cloak and was now standing in a red, woollen shirt with very long sleeves hanging down from his hands, and with naked feet. He hit his chest with his naked arms. One of his arms was crippled; he had probably mutilated it himself at some time. His mouth was a wound full of blood; recently he must have cut off his lips. It was as if his white teeth were grinning; it was terrible to behold. His mouth opened and blood poured out, his eyes were rolling, and the veins on his forehead were swollen. The movements became more and more violent, though none of them moved their feet from the ground. The dancers seemed not to be humans, but machines, they did not any longer pronounce the words, but turned them into short howls. It was like a death moan; it was terrible; the more I watched the dance, the more I felt that I was in an asylum for lunatics. The man beside me whispered: 'For god's sake, do not laugh, they will kill us!' 'Laugh?' I answered, 'I think I am going to cry! It is shocking, it is terrible! I cannot stand it any more!' I said and moved towards the exit, and in the same moment a couple of the dancers fainted and fell to the ground. (Andersen 1944, pp. 251-252, my translation).

The next day Andersen went to witness the Mevlevi ceremony, and seems to have been relieved because, as he said (p. 254, my translation):

There was nothing terrifying about this dance. One could almost call it elegant, but you would have to forget they were people, and rather think they were dolls. Combined with the faint, monotonous music, the dance gave the whole thing an atmosphere of a quiet madness which was rather moving than frightening. The whole performance could hardly be called morally constructive; it seemed to me like a ballet, whereas the dance of the Howling Dervishes remained in my memory as the image of a lunatic asylum.

Hamsun's report on the howling dervishes is more like a farce; he ridicules the ceremony, of which he of course understands nothing. However, there is no malice in his description, and the overall impression it gives is extremely funny (1976, pp.

280-284). The contrast with Andersen's frightened account is quite striking. There are elements in Hamsun's account that could have their origin in Gautier's report (1990, pp. 144-148), but Hamsun's fascination is quite genuine, as becomes also clear from his statement that later on during his stay he went back and visited the *tekke* of the Howling Dervishes again.[7]

## A Glimpse of the Sultan

Another 'must' for travellers to Istanbul seems to have been to get a glimpse of the Sultan. Rålamb and other envoys were of course received by the Grand Vizier and the Sultan in audiences; in the nineteenth century, however, foreign visitors, especially, it seems, private persons of a certain standing, could secure the opportunity to witness the Sultan's procession to Friday prayer. Andersen watches this event in the street close by the Hagia Sophia mosque as the Topkapı Sarayı was still the residence of the sultans at that time; at Hamsun's time, the procession goes to the Yıldız Mosque, and foreign visitors were directed to a roof overlooking the garden. Andersen concentrates on the visual impression of the procession, and when the Sultan himself comes, the 19-year-old Abdülmecid, he describes him thus (1944, p. 265, my translation):

> He was looking very pale and thin, his features showed suffering, and his dark eyes looked staringly at the spectators, especially at the Franks. We took our hats off and saluted him. The soldiers shouted 'Long live the Emperor', but he did nothing to greet them back. 'Why does he not greet us?' I asked a young Turk beside me. 'He saw we took off our hats, didn't he?' 'He looked at you', the Turk said, 'He looked at you very closely.' We should be content with that, that was equal to a greeting. I told the Turk that all Frankish rulers greet their people by removing their hats in the same way as we greet him. That seemed to him like a fairy-tale.

Hamsun's report on the Sultan, however (1976, pp. 285-294), is much more interesting because of his very personal interpretation of his appearance. The Sultan at that time was Abdülhamid II, the most feared and despised of all the rulers since the middle of the seventeenth century because of his despotism and partly because of his paranoid disposition. No contemporary foreign sources speak positively about him, and since his death he has, more or less with good reason, become the symbol of the

---

[7] Other aspects of the visits by these Scandinavian travellers to the dervish ceremonies have been treated by me in Brendemoen 1988b.

oppressive aspect of the Ottoman Empire. Hamsun, however, is fascinated by the look of the Sultan (p. 292, my translation):

> What was terrible about this man? The cunning, the horrible aspect of him, where was it, and where was the murderer? His brown eyes pleased me because of their open and lenient look. He was looking tired. He responded in an Asiatic indifferent way to the salute of the troops. But even this salute is something he has personally adopted; his predecessor, Abdülaziz, never returned a salute. Maybe this little act should be subtracted from his bestial nature and added to his human one. I recently read that Abdülhamid is so nervous and stressed that he has to have knives lying around his bed during night. His wife moved in her sleep, and the Sultan was so horrified that he took one of the knives and plunged into her. It is just as if the Turkish Sultan had memorised an excellent Norwegian saying that at slaughtering time when you have a lot of sausages, one more or less is just a trifle. He has 299 wives left, does he not; just give me another!

Both Andersen and Hamsun seem to have missed two interesting aspects of the procession to the Friday mosque, first why it was so important to have this public ceremony every week; and the special interest shown by the female spectators. The first point is mentioned both by Gautier (1990, p. 175) and by de Amicis, an Italian traveller whose report on Istanbul from 1877, which has now (2005) appeared in a new translation into English, is most probably the best travel book about Istanbul ever written (p. 140):

> … indeed the Sultan appears punctually every Friday in order to give his people proof of his existence, since several times in the past a sultan's natural or violent death has been kept secret by some court conspiracy.

The other point is the relatively large proportion of women, mostly foreign tourists, present at the ceremony, which is explained directly by Gautier (1990, p. 178):

> Je donnais le bras à une jeune dame italienne qui m'avait prié de l'accompagner, et qui se penchait avidement à travers le haie pour contempler les traits du sultan; car un homme qui a seize cents concubines est un phénomène qui intéresse au plus haut degré la curiosité des femmes.[8]

---

[8] 'I offered my arm to the young Italian lady who had asked me to accompany her, and who was leaning eagerly against the fence in order to examine the features of the sultan, for a man who has sixteen hundred concubines is a phenomenon which is of extreme interest to the curiosity of women.'

## The Turks

When it comes to the impression the nineteenth-century travellers had of the Turks, Andersen is remarkably silent on this point; the reason is probably that he was so dazzled by the mixture of races and peoples in the streets and bazaars of Istanbul that he was not quite aware of who were Turks, who were Armenians, and who were Greeks. Hamsun, however, had very clear views about the different elements of Istanbul's population. His dislike of the Jews, which was to become fatal in his later life, is already very clear at this stage, but he also shows a strong dislike of Greeks and Armenians, which is balanced only by a profound liking of the Turks, with a special emphasis on their pride. Talking about tourist guides, for example, he says (1976, p. 272, my translation):

> A Turk is no tourist guide. He is prouder than that; he knows that his people had the highest culture at the time when the Romans were still barbarians. The tourist guides are Greeks, Armenians and Jews. The Turk is a boatman, rows his kaique, he is a porter and a day labourer, but he is not a tourist guide.

Hamsun's admiration of the pride of the Turks becomes evident several times in his description. The reader is almost reminded about the much later, very famous story about Atatürk, who had invited the British ambassador to the presidential palace. He had arranged beforehand that one of his servants should carry a huge tray full of glasses, and then stumble so that the tray fell on the floor and all the glasses broke. Whereupon Atatürk turned to the British ambassador and said, 'You see, *Türkten kul olmaz*, the Turks cannot become servants', or: 'The Turks do not become slaves.'

Alongside the pride of the Turks, Hamsun is fascinated by their Oriental capacity for keeping impenetrable poker faces and not revealing their feelings. In an historical essay following his travel report, most probably written with the help of encyclopaedias and newspaper articles after he returned home (pp. 303-311), he deplores the decline of the Ottoman Empire and speculates on the effect the defeats in the Balkans must have had on the Turks as a nation. This is quite different from the chapter on the Turks as individuals in the de Amicis book. Much of the difference may be explained by the military defeats that had taken place in the years between de Amicis' visit in 1874 (and the publication of his book in 1877) and Hamsun's visit in 1899 (and publication in 1905), which indeed may have triggered a change of mentality that must have reached its zenith with defeat in the First World War. If we disregard the racial stereotyping, which seems to have been quite acceptable at the time of both de Amicis and Hamsun, it is very interesting to observe that de Amicis, after having commented on the inexpressive, inscrutable faces of the Turks, 'revealing nothing of their souls or minds' (p. 269), and praising their physical beauty and cleanliness, suddenly interrupts himself, stating (p. 271):

> But this is only on the surface. The rottenness lies within. The corruption is hidden by the separation of the two sexes, idleness is masked by calm, dignity conceals pride, the composed gravity of countenance – which seems to indicate thoughtfulness – is only produced by a deadly intellectual inertia, and their apparent temperance is nothing but an absence of life in its true sense.

Further on he ascribes this mentality partly to a feeling of contempt caused by the fact that the Turks have been rulers of a considerable part of the world for several centuries (p. 273):

> Thus they not only despise European civilisation as vacuous, they fear it as hostile; and since they may not subdue it by force, they oppose it with the intractable resistance of their inertia.

Although the last statement may be partly true for some reactionary circles in Turkey even today, the people described by de Amicis in his gross generalisations is totally different from the Turks of today, who seem to have gone through a profound Europeanisation process, at least in Istanbul. The inscrutable faces belong to the past, and apart from the melancholy tendencies elaborated by Pamuk, today's Istanbullus are quite indistinguishable from Greeks and Italians. If we do not completely disregard de Amicis' description as racist, prejudiced and reactionary, we may perhaps interpret the picture given by Hamsun as an intermediate stage in a development towards Europeanisation. Pamuk ascribes the melancholy of present-day Turks to the fact that the Ottoman Empire was defeated in the First World War, but if we think of the Westernisation process that was accelerated after this defeat and the very conscious efforts made by Atatürk to turn Turkey into a European country, and also the change of mentality that has taken place in most circles and social strata in Turkey, we may be quite certain that the doors of the EU would have been closed even more tightly than they are if the attitude described by de Amicis had still been prevalent today.

# Bibliography

Andersen, Hans Christian, *En Digters bazar* (*Romaner og Rejseskildringer*, vol. 6), (Copenhagen, 1944).

Brendemoen, Bernt, 'Some remarks on Claes Brodersson Rålamb and his contemporaries', in *Turcica et orientalia — Studies in honour of Gunnar Jarring* (*Swedish Research Institute in Istanbul – Transactions*, vol. 1), (Stockholm 1988a), pp. 9-18.

Brendemoen, Bernt, 'İskandinav seyyahları göziyle dervişlik ve tarikat' ['Dervishes and religious orders seen through the eyes of Scandinavian travellers'], in *1. Milletlerarası Mevlâna kongresi – First international Mevlana congress* (Konya, 3-5 May 1987), Tebliğler, (Konya: Selçuk Üniversitesi 1988b), pp. 259-269.

Callmer, Christian, *In Orientem. Svenskars färder och forskningar i den europeiska och asiatiska Orienten under 1700-talet (Asiatica Suecana, 2)*, (Stockholm: Almqvist & Wiksell International, 1985).

*Conrad Jacob Hiltebrandt's Dreifache Gesandschaftsreise nach Siebenbürgen, der Ukraine und Constantinopel (1656-1658), (Historiska Handlingar, 30:2.).* Herausgegeben und erläutert von Franz Babinger (Leiden, 1937).

de Amicis, Edmondo, *Constantinople* (London: Hesperus, 2005).

de Busbecq, Oghier Ghiselin, *The Turkish Letters*, translated and edited by E.S. Foster (Oxford: University Press, 1927, 1968).

Gautier, Théophile, *Constantinople. Istanbul en 1852* (Istanbul: Isis, 1990).

Hamsun, Knut, 'Under Halvmaanen', in *Stridende Liv*, (Christiania, 1905). (The quotations in my article refer to the 1976 edition of his *Samlede verker* (Complete Works), vol. 4.

Pamuk, Orhan, *Istanbul – Hatıralar ve Şehir* (Istanbul: Yapı Kredi Yayınları, 2003).

Rålamb, Claes, *Diarium under resa till Konstantinopel 1657-1658*. Utgivet av Kungl. Samfundet för utgifvande af handskrifter rörande Skandinaviens historia genom Christian Callmer (*Historiska Handlingar* 37:3), (Stockholm, 1963).

Wallich, Johann Ulrich, *Religio Turcica: Mahometis vita. Et orientalis cum occidentali Antichristo Comparatio* (Stade, 1659).

Ådahl, Karin (ed.), *Minnet av Konstantinopel. Den osmansk-turkiska 1700-talssamlingen på Biby* (Stockholm: Atlantis, 2003).

Ådahl, Karin (ed.), *The Sultan's Procession. The Swedish embassy to Sultan Mehmet IV in 1657-1658 and the Rålamb paintings* (Istanbul: Swedish Research Institute, 2006).

# The Turks in Norwegian Legends

## Narratives and Function of Stereotypes in a Historical Setting

Ann Helene Bolstad Skjelbred

## Introduction

The present public debate in Norway shows a growing opposition to guest workers and political and other refugees. Although the percentage of dark-skinned people from countries with religions, languages and cultures completely different from our own is very low compared to the immigration of people of white, Western nationalities, the debate has mainly concentrated on people from Africa and Asia and their characteristics compared to characteristics of our own people and culture. In many communities people have expressed fear that the Muslim religion will gain dominance over the existing Lutheranism. In a country where around 85 per cent of the people are members of the State Lutheran Church there is a strongly rooted scepticism towards any other religion. The fear of people with physical, cultural and religious traits different from the dominating Norwegian ones has also led to expressions of racism. Historically, this fear of people with different skin colourings, and with facial and behavioural characteristics different from the dominant characteristics of Norwegians is not recent, although Norway has been a fairly homogenous society compared to most of the European continent. One example is the folk tradition about the Turks.

In popular Norwegian and literary narratives from the 1800s, we find the expression 'snout-Turk'.[1] This is a dialect expression for Turks who were considered to have mouths like a pig's snout. The word is still known in Norwegian dialects but

---

[1] Snout-turk = tryntyrken.

without the extreme connotations. The Swedish equivalent is 'dog'-Turk.² A significant and horrifying feature of the folk narratives is that the Turks ate human flesh. In a Norwegian diary from 1313 it is told that people believed that two Turks staying in Bergen bought human flesh and blood by the barrel, paying one or two pieces of gold per barrel.³ In popular belief the Turks were feared for their extreme cruelty. Perhaps this is a general and long-lasting opinion in the Western world. In sociological tests in the 1930s American students were asked to rate characteristics of ethnic groups. The Turks were characterised as cruel, very religious, treacherous, sensual, ignorant and physically dirty.⁴ The test was one of many in continuing research into stereotypes.

## Stereotypes and Identity

The concept of a stereotype is taken from the technology of printing, but the term originated in everyday language in the social sciences and has been widely used without ever being precisely defined. However, when a concept is referred to as a stereotype, the implication is that it is simple rather than complex or differentiated; it is erroneous rather than accurate; it has been acquired second-hand rather than through direct experience with the reality it is supposed to represent; and it is resistant to modification by new experience.⁵ The components of stereotypes may be physical traits such as skin-colour, hair etc. But far more conspicuous are personality and intellectual traits, taken to be transmitted through behaviour. Traits represented in stereotypes depend solely upon properties which a group of people agree are typical of a class. In this sense, the properties of stereotypes have a social reality, regardless of whether objective measurement would support them or not.⁶

Stereotypes are indications of group-belongingness. They not only enable people to manage their interpersonal and group relations, but by holding such stereotypes they symbolically expresses their group identifications.⁷ Stereotypes are therefore vital elements in creating group identities. To create 'pictures' of strangers is an important part of creating 'pictures' of oneself and thereby creating identity. This can be done on any level: between social classes, ethnic groups, races, sexes etc.⁸ The strangeness is made visible through different components considered culturally

---

² Dog-turk = hundturken.
³ Pavels 1888, p. 245.
⁴ Harding 1968, p. 260.
⁵ Harding 1868, p. 259.
⁶ Vinacke 1957, pp. 238-239.
⁷ Fishman 1956, pp. 39-40.
⁸ See the different contributions in Gerndt 1988.

significant; names, food, clothes, physical characteristics and behaviour can all be bases for stereotyping. When people are asked to list characteristics of another group as well as their own, experiments in the social sciences show that socially desirable characteristics are more likely to be emphasised in a group's description of itself, while undesirable characteristics are more likely to be emphasised in the description of a group by members of another group.[9] In popular narratives, however, the favourable description of oneself and of one's own group is often not verbalised. It has to be understood indirectly.

## Folk Narratives

While social scientists have been occupied with the concept of the stereotype and of the question of why people stereotype, folk narratives are a lucid example of how stereotypes can be expressed and transmitted. The study of personal narratives has shown that attitudes are often expressed through stories rather than through plain statements. At one level, therefore, folk narratives constitute an active component in transmitting stereotypes, although it is not clear which level it is. It may be that stereotypes that seem to be more or less authorised do not need narratives for support, but they may be used actively in continuing conflicts or where the validity of the stereotypes is questioned.

Norwegians are historically a nation of seafarers. The fear of the Turks can be seen in stories about controversies between Norwegian sailors and North African pirates. The legends do not discriminate when it comes to geography, though. In one legend about a man from the northern part of Norway on his way to Bergen with a cargo, it is told that he was taken captive by the Turks on the western coast of Norway. Legends about heroic Norwegians often say that the sailors were held captive by the 'snout'-Turks. Not only were they fed well as preparation for being slaughtered, they were also used as plough-horses. In light of recent historical research about Danish, Norwegian and Icelandic sailors kidnapped and brought to Algeria, Morocco or Tunisia, the legends retell genuine factual experiences.

Literarily, one of Norway's great authors has used the motif that the legendary king Charles the Great used 'snout'-Turks in his army. Moreover, in an historical legend it is told that the Scot George Sinclair brought a 'snout'-Turk with him on his military campaign in Norway in 1611-1613. This legendary trait is connected to the belief that the Turks had a dog's sense of smell and to deceive him, the Norwegians had to hide in a field of hemp.

---

[9] Harding 1968, pp. 260-261.

In an historical legend from Valdres, a valley in the southern part of Norway, this dramatic event is said to have occurred some time before 1800. A highly respected son of one of the farmers in the district often went to Christiania, the name of the Norwegian capital at that time, bringing farmers' goods for sale. At the marketplace the young man was approached by a distinguished lady who wanted him to bring a barrel of butter to her house. On arriving there he was well received and shown through one room after another until he was finally nicely seated and entertained with fine liquor, offered one glass after another. The man was wise enough to pour the liquor down into his heavy scarf instead of drinking it. Pretending to be very drunk he let himself fall to the floor. The door opened and a man appeared carrying a tray with sharpened knives and a silver bowl for collecting the blood. The Norwegian then jumped up, beat the intruder, wrecked the house and left it in a shambles. The house was said to be owned by a 'snout'-Turk. A variant on this legend states that the house was a slaughterhouse where innocent people were lured inside and killed. The meat was then shipped to Turkey where people were said to eat human flesh. The same motif is found in the legend about a young farm girl in service at a rich farmer's house where she was treated very nicely with lots of good food. However, after the child of the house remarked that she felt sorry for the servant girl who was going to be slaughtered, she understood both the reason for the good food and for the farmer's hugs and caresses.

The cannibalistic characteristics of the Turks added to the opinion that they were heathen. This is a trait characterising the Turks in a legend (collected in the first part of the 1800s) about a sailor who came home to Norway after many years, having been held in captivity by the Turks. He was considered to have acquired the Turks' heathen habits, shown by the fact that he kept his cap on in church!

That the opinion of the Turks was not merely a legendary motif is also demonstrated in rumours that were acted upon. In a recent private publication it is told that rumours about a local north-Norwegian merchant in partnership with the Turks were so hard to kill off that in 1839 the merchant had to put an advertisement in a newspaper to disavow them.[10] A parallel illustration of legends coming to life took place in Christiania in 1869. According to the rumours, the Turks had made a deal with the Freemasons to supply the Turks with human flesh. The Freemasons then lured young and innocent girls into their houses, slaughtered them and shipped the meat to Turkey. The rumours resulted in a demonstration directed against the Freemasons' house in downtown Christiania. The folk belief in a conspiracy between the Turks and the Freemasons has been the subject of a Swedish empirical study (Bergstrand

---

[10] Andersen 2006, p. 104.

1956). A result of the demonstration in 1869 was a series of broadside ballads, which have been documented in an article by the late Norwegian folklorist Reidar Christiansen (1932). One of the broadside ballads has this heading: 'Today a new song is published about the "snout"-Turk who dresses like any decent Norwegian to dupe young and pretty girls whom he kidnaps, slaughters and salts.' The broadside ballad clearly make fun of the incident and of course of the folk belief about the Turks and the Freemasons. But the broadside ballad, the legends and the rumours can be seen as indications of how one's identity is indirectly pictured in contrast to somebody else. This is done by stereotyping.

The structuralist theory of binary oppositions gives a fruitful insight into how stereotyping of others in fact means an identification of the self. The Norwegian folklorist Stein Mathisen has applied this theory to show the dynamics of an ethnic classification through an analysis of the folklore around the Lapps. Narratives symbolically built on oppositions such as animal and human, nature and culture are used to draw the cultural ethnic borderline between the Lapps and the Norwegians (Mathisen 1983). The classification of another ethnic group can be seen as a structural opposition to a classification of one's own where the characterisation of the self and one's own group seems to be a silent assumption. Moreover, the worse the adversary group is pictured the more glorified one's own group will look.

While the Turk's features are characterised by a derogatory description classifying him with animals, the silent assumption is of course that such a classification is not valid for the Norwegian. Moreover, both the legends and the broadside ballads depict the Turks as deceitful, they (or in league with Freemasons, merchants or a 'fine lady') lure young girls or other honest people by simple tricks such as dressing up like any nice Norwegian or inviting innocent youngsters into their houses under false pretences. Worst of all, the Turks have cannibalistic traits; they slaughter people and eat human flesh. The legends tell how the young Norwegian male heroically fights his way out of the house and is saved.

The folklore around the 'snout'-Turk shows that this binary opposition is created not only on the differences between nationalities and cultures as different as the Turks and the Norwegians. The stereotyping of the Turks is active as identification on the level of ethnicity. But the legends are also used to create identity in opposition to other groups of people. The legends tell of the young farmer going to town where he comes into contact with deceitful city people; the opposition between country people and city people is underscored. The legend telling of the man approached by a lady who invites him into her house under false pretences, and the legend about the girl in the rich farmer's service, underscore the opposition between the lower and upper social classes. In the 1800s Norway was rapidly developing from being mainly a country of fishermen and farmers in small communities to a nation of commerce and industry and growing cities with lurking dangers on every street corner. The safe country life is a silent assumption, in contrast to the dangerous city life.

The linkage between the Turks and the Freemasons points to a very interesting opposition, but it is difficult to see how the Freemasons had come to play such an important role as expressions of social fear. The first Norwegian order of Freemasons was established in 1749 but the number of individual members was small in the 1800s and at that time they were limited to only a few cities in Norway. In the legends I therefore see them only as an extension of the Turks and not in the role of independent antagonists to the lower social classes.

## Conclusion

The folklore and the folk narratives of the 'snout'-Turks may today be viewed as curious examples of people's ridiculous beliefs or merely as humorous stories without any connection to either beliefs or real life. On the other hand they can also be interpreted as serious expressions of social fear, the fear of strangers and of different social groups. In addition, as the legends invariably picture the Turk, the rich farmer or city people as the antagonists and the losers and the Norwegian sailor or country man or woman as the winner, they can be seen as expressions of stereotypes of another group with silent assumptions about one's own group in the process of creating identity.

## Bibliography

Andersen, L. J., *'Røvar-Alexander' og barken 'Patriot'* (Leknes, 2006).

Bergstrand, C.-M., *Frimurarna och hundturken. Vad folk trott om frimurarna* (Göteborg, 1913).

Christiansen, R., 'Albrechtsons visesamling', in Universitetsbiblioteket i Oslo, *Festskrift til Den Norske Avdeling 1882-1932* (Oslo, 1932), pp. 106-130.

Fishman, J. A., 'An examination of the process and function of social stereotyping', *Journal of Social Psychology,* 43 (1956), pp. 27-64.

Gerndt, H. (ed.): *Stereotypvorstellungen im Alltagsleben. Beitrage zum Themenkreis Fremdbilder – Selbstbilder – Identitat. Festschrift fur Georg R. Schroubek zum 65. Geburtstag* (München, 1988).

Harding, J., 'Stereotypes', in D. Sills (ed.), *International Encyclopaedia of the Social Sciences* 1-17 (New York, 1968).

Mathisen, S., *'Det er forskjell på folk og finner.' En analyse av etnisk kategorisering i fortellertradisjonen. Magistergradsavhandling i folkloristikk* (Bergen: Etnofolkloristisk institutt, 1983).

Pavels, C., *Dagbøger for Aarene 1812-1813* (Kristiania, 1888).

Vinacke, W E., 'Stereotypes as social concepts', *Journal of Social Psychology,* 46 (1957), pp. 229-243.

# An Islamic Road to Europe?

## On the Political Role of Religion in Turkey

Bjørn Olav Utvik

It would seem like a paradox: of the Muslim majority countries that formerly belonged to the Ottoman Empire, Turkey is (with the possible exception of Albania) supposedly today the most thoroughly secularised country, a result of a conscious policy vigorously pursued by the state at least since the mid-1920s. Yet at the same time it is the only one with a government and a parliamentary majority based on an Islamist party. Perhaps it is no coincidence that it is also, despite its shortcomings, the only democracy.

Indeed the relationship of the Turkish Republic to religion is something of an enigma. In 1993 a representative of the Turkish embassy in Oslo, talking to students at the University of Oslo, declared emphatically that she did not know anything about Islam, since religion was not important in Turkey. Yet minutes later when questioned about the war raging in Bosnia the same person replied: 'This is of deep concern to us, especially since the Bosnians are our fellow Muslims'!

In an effort to make sense of this paradox and to estimate its significance for the future developments of Turkey's relationship with Europe, the present essay will briefly review some aspects of Turkish history with an emphasis on the role of religion in Ottoman and in particular republican times. This will provide the basis for reflection on the current role of religion in Turkish politics and how this relates to Turkey's effort to gain entry into the European Union.

## From Gazi State to Secular Republic

The beginnings of the Turkish presence, and indeed Turkish statehood, in present-day Turkey, can be dated to the Battle of Manzikert in 1071, where the conquering Seljuks under Alp Arslan defeated the Byzantine army and captured the Emperor Romanus, thereby opening the gateway to Anatolia for invading Turkish tribes. For nine-tenths of its history the legitimacy of this statehood has been intimately and explicitly linked to religion.

The Seljuks themselves had recently emerged out of Central Asia and marched westwards with the declared intention of liberating the Caliph in Baghdad, the symbolic leader of all Muslims and indeed of the *Dar al-Islam,* from the deviant Shia rulers holding sway since the mid-tenth century. Having captured Baghdad in 1055 they then proceeded to take up the holy cause of fighting the infidels of Constantinople. Later, during and after the vicissitudes of the crusades and the Mongol invasions, the Anatolian part of the Seljuk empire split up into a number of statelets dominated by various Turkish tribes. These statelets came to be known as the Gazi states, a 'Gazi' (from the Arabic *ghazi*) being the closest Muslim equivalent of a crusader, i.e. one engaged in military struggle against the enemies of the faith.

The most successful of these Gazi states was the one named after one of its earliest rulers, Osman (ruled 1281-1324). In 1453 Osman's successor and descendant in the sixth generation Mehmet II[1] finally realised that age-old goal of the Muslims when he conquered the Christian capital of the East and remade it into Istanbul, the new capital of an empire that soon came to straddle the three continents of Africa, Asia and Europe.

It is sometimes stated that Islam differs from Christianity in that the religion founded by the Prophet Muhammad never knew any division between religion and politics. This statement is quite problematic. One reason is that in pre-modern times the general differentiation of society was to say the least much less pronounced than today. Among other things this meant that whether in a Muslim, Christian or other cultural setting, at the time when the Ottoman Empire was established, the emergence of religion as a separate sphere that might thrive in isolation from social life, politics, and the economy was at best in an embryonic stage. Even in the West it was only slowly, and for a long time only within the narrow social stratum of the elite, that religion ceased to provide the framework within which both society and nature was understood. Another reason is that if we look at the relationship between religion and politics from an *institutional* point of view, Islamic states were never ruled by the clergy. Certainly the caliphs, sultans and emirs always kept learned men of religion, *ulama,* by their sides who could provide religious legitimacy for their actions, and religiously trained scholars were appointed to the main positions in the judiciary. Yet the bulk of the *ulama* typically kept their distance from the state, seeking to fund their schools and mosques from independently controlled donated property, and to act as custodians of morality, criticising state actions from an independent vantage point.

---

[1] 'Mehmet' is the Turkish version of the name Muhammad.

What *remains* true, though, is that as the Islamic mode of government took shape over the centuries, it solved the question of the relations of religion and government in its own distinct way. This way obviously has something to do with the heritage of the Prophet, who unlike Jesus in his own lifetime became a statesman as well as a proclaimed messenger from God. In the Sunni tradition, to which the Ottomans emphatically adhered, the caliphs who succeeded the Prophet as leaders of the nascent Islamic community were *not* considered to be directly inspired by God, yet they retained the total of the Prophet's earthly tasks of leadership: from leadership in prayer to leadership in war. As later the position of caliph faded into symbolic insignificance, real power passed to the *sultan*, literally 'the power', in practice the general or tribal leader commanding the strongest military force. However, theoretically on behalf of the caliph, the sultan was supposed to continue exercising the earthly functions of the Prophet, which included ensuring that Islamic law, the *Sharia*, was enforced in the country, that communal prayers were held every Friday, and that the pilgrimage to Mecca remained safe.

When the Ottoman state established itself as an empire it went further than earlier Muslim states in creating a centralised hierarchy of Islamic clerics closely tied to the state. This became particularly accentuated after the capture of Constantinople, when the sultan seemed inclined to emulate the caesaro-papist government of the Byzantines. The clerical hierarchy was headed by the position of Sheyhüleslam, or Grand Mufti, in Constantinople who was charged with assuring the observation of the sacred law in Ottoman territories and supervising the activities of the Sharia judges. The Sheyhülislam was simultaneously one of the highest officers of the state, directly below the sultan himself, and on a par with the leaders of the military and civilian bureaucracy.[2]

At least since the conquest of the Egyptian-based Mamluk Empire in 1517 the Ottoman sultan also laid claim to the title of caliph, successor of the Prophet and leader of all Muslims of the world. The last Abbasid caliph, residing at the Mamluk court and possessing absolutely no powers, is said to have surrendered his powers to the sultan. For the Ottomans the immediate purpose was probably to gain legitimacy for the wars of expansion against another Muslim states, which could now be presented as the putting down of rebellions against the legitimate leader of the Muslim world. Incidentally it meant that for the first time since the early tenth century the position of caliph was claimed by the one holding actual military and political power. Nevertheless the title was only intermittently used until the late eighteenth century when it was activated in order to rally Muslim support for the fight against intruding

---

[2] Joseph Schacht, *An Introduction to Islamic Law* (Oxford: Clarendon Press, 1964), p. 90.

European powers. Under the rule of Abdülhamid II (1876-1908), a period known as the Hamidian despotism, the claim to the caliphate was put in the foreground of Ottoman propaganda as part of a wider return to an Islamic legitimacy after the flirt with European ideologies in the 1860s and early 1870s. Despite the fall of Abdülhamid in 1908 and the accession to power of the modernist reformers in the Committee for Union and Progress (better known as the Young Turks), the caliphal pretension was activated again in the First World War. In November 1914 the Sultan in his capacity as Caliph declared a *jihad* against Britain and France, implying that it was a duty for all Muslims worldwide to support Turkey in the war.[3]

This war resulted in the collapse of the empire, and the Sultan-Caliph, having signed the humiliating Treaty of Sèvres in 1920, was brushed aside by the popular War of Independence led by Mustafa Kemal, later to be known as Atatürk. Kemal proceeded to establish the Republic of Turkey in 1923 and in the years that followed instituted comprehensive changes under the banner of separation of religion and state, known in Turkish as the principle of *laiklik*, from the French *laïcité*. Yet the very War of Independence that made Kemal's reputation and established his enormous reservoir of legitimacy, was fought precisely under the banner of Islam. He proudly donned the title of Gazi Mustafa Kemal, i.e. a fighter for the sake of Islam against the unbelievers. The call was for the Muslims to unite against the infidel invaders from Greece, who with the consent of the major powers had taken Izmir in 1919, and were pressing further into Western Anatolia. In a declaration to the people on behalf of the Grand National Assembly he had established, Mustafa Kemal stated in 1921:

> We, your representative, swear in the name of God and the Prophet that this is not a rebellion against the sultan or the caliph. Do not believe the lies of those English spies who want to make our sacred country defenceless and deserted. They are trying to turn you against your brothers who gave their lives for the honour of their country and religion. If you help them, religion will lose its last homeland, and our nation its freedom… May God curse those traitors who help the enemy, and may His praise be upon those who strive to save the caliph and the sultan, the Nation and the Fatherland.[4]

In line with this the nationalists demanded of the Western powers occupying Istanbul and dictating the post-war settlement that an independent state be created within the territories of Muslim majority population. When after the new Treaty of Lausanne

---

[3] Erik J. Zürcher, *Turkey: A Modern History* (London: I.B. Tauris, 1997), p. 119.
[4] Quoted here from Camilla T. Nereid, *In the Light of Said Nursi: Turkish Nationalism and the Religious Alternative* (Bergen: Centre for Middle Eastern and Islamic Studies, 1997), p. 114.

An Islamic Road to Europe?

in 1923 the Turkish state was established roughly within its present borders, it was agreed that a population exchange take place with Greece, so that Greeks be moved from Turkey to Greece, and Turks in the opposite direction. But the criterion was based on religion. A Turkish-speaking Christian was considered to be a Greek and had to leave Turkey. The same applied to Greek-speaking Muslims in Greece with some exceptions. Today paradoxically secular Turkey has one of the world's most homogeneously Muslim populations; around 99 per cent are Muslims.

When the Sultan was deposed in 1922, Kemal installed another Ottoman prince in a purely ceremonial function as Caliph. But by 1924 the caliphate had already been finally abolished. While this act may have had multiple motives, among them making clear that the new state had no territorial or other ambitions vis-à-vis the wider Muslim world, and in particular the Arab parts of it, it marked the beginning of a wave of reforms designed to minimise the role of religion and religious leaders in the public sphere in Turkey.

After a major rebellion in 1925 in the Kurdish areas, led by the Sufi leader Sheikh Sait and triggered by protest against the abolition of the caliphate, Mustafa Kemal forced through the Grand National Assembly a 'Law on the Maintenance of Power' which remained in force until 1929. This law enabled the government to shut down all opposition activity, and Turkey was turned into an authoritarian single-party state. With all opponents silenced the Kemalists rushed through a series of reforms. One of the first steps taken was to forbid the activities of the Sufi orders, the *tarikat*, which played a pivotal role in popular religiosity as well as social life throughout the country. In 1925 a law on clothing prohibited the use of the turban and the fez and made it obligatory for Turkish men to wear a European-style hat. In 1926 Sharia courts were abolished and the whole range of legislation was exchanged for new laws based on European models. The same year the solar Gregorian calendar was substituted for the Muslim lunar one. Finally in 1928 the Latin alphabet was introduced for the writing of Turkish, while the use of Arabic letters (not to mention the Arabic language) was prohibited, to the extent that the Koran had to be studied in Turkish and the prayer call made in Turkish. The same year the reference to Islam as the religion of the state was dropped from the constitution. Linked to this whole process was the removal of religion from public school curricula and the closing down of the traditional institutions of religious learning, the *medreses*.[5]

Nevertheless what took place was very far from an institutional separation of the state from religion. Religion became if anything more intimately integrated into the

---

[5] For an overview of Kemal's secularising reforms see Yildiz Atasoy, *Turkey, Islamists and Democracy: Tradition and Globalization in a Muslim State* (London: Tauris, 2005), pp. 36 ff.

state apparatus than ever before. But from a position where religion had a central place in the legitimation of the state and where its clerical leaders held place of pride in government, Islam was relegated to a subordinate department of the bureaucracy. The intention was to control religion so tightly that it could never become the platform for opposition to the ruling elite and its ideology. In 1924, on the abolition of the caliphate, Kemal's government established the Directorate for Religious Affairs, most often simply known as the *Diyanet*. Since then this institution has endeavoured to control the teaching, preaching and practice of Islam within the country and even among the large Turkish diaspora in Europe. In fact what took place may well be described as a 'one-way secularisation' where the state rid itself of religious control while reinforcing its own control over religion. Perhaps the crux of the matter is that the core intention was not the institutional separation of the two spheres, but removing religious influence from the public sphere altogether. To do so religious institutions and organisations could not be allowed to function independently of the state; on the contrary there was a pressing need to control and often suppress religious manifestations. It is striking and somewhat ironic in this regard that the self-proclaimed staunchly secularist Turkish state took it upon itself to tell the people what constituted true Islam, and what fell outside its scope. This reached the point in 1964 where the reformist thinker and activist Said Nursi (see below), was proclaimed by a declaration of the Diyanet to be spreading heresy.[6]

In retrospect the following picture emerges: the Ottoman state had historically based its legitimacy on its defence of Islam against a hostile outer world, and on sustaining Islamic practice within, notably basing its judicial system on the Islamic Sharia law. Through modernising reforms initiated in the eighteenth century a new educated elite emerged, which contrary to the traditional intellectual elite of the Islamic schools, the *medrese*s, had received a modern European-inspired schooling. In its effort to mould the state and society in its own image, this new elite eventually came to opt for a secular Turkish nationalism in order to set themselves free from the limits of the Ottoman traditions so tightly bound up with and, not least, legitimised by reference to religion. While this intention was already clearly visible in the Young Turk revolution of 1908, in order to mobilise the population during the World War and again in the War of Resistance of 1919-1922, the modernising elite saw no other option than to make appeals to Islam, the deeply held belief of the masses. In fact, religion also played a vital part in defining the nation upon which the new state would be built: all Muslims were considered Turks; Christians irrespective of language were not.[7]

---

[6] Nereid, op. cit., pp. 65 ff.
[7] Soner Cagaptay, *Islam, Secularism, and Nationalism in Modern Turkey: Who is a Turk?* (London: Routledge, 2006), p. 156.

Nevertheless, when victory was achieved, the new masters of the state switched to an aggressive secularist agenda, in particular after the uprising of 1925. But despite the wish to remove religion from the sphere of public debate and decision-making, so shortly after religion had been used to mobilise the people and to decide the burning question 'Who is a Turk?', it was thought impossible to let religion loose, as it were. So the Diyanet was set up to rein religion in instead.

The paradox referred to initially of Turkey's simultaneous detachment from and attachment to Islam was therefore built into the foundation of the republic. The dilemmas inherent in a state project *de facto* built on the idea of a unified nation defined by its religious affiliation, yet strongly committed to keeping this same religion away from political life, is something Turkey shares with states like Israel and Pakistan.

## A Double Loneliness

One result of the authoritarian secularisation from above was a double sense of loneliness. On the one hand, through the ban on the *tarikat*, the Turks were deprived of the religious organisations that used to provide a comforting religious framework and vital social solidarity for everyday life for a vast majority among them. 'Each individual was thus left on his own.'[8] On the other hand the Turks were alone in that they had been cut off both from their own past, and from their Muslim Middle Eastern neighbourhood (incidentally without gaining much in friendly relations with their neighbours on the other side, the Greeks). They became as one expression had it, 'a nation of forgetters'.

For a visitor to major Turkish cities this cultural loneliness is acutely felt, in what one might term the 'absent presence' of the Ottoman heritage. In particular walking through Istanbul the past grandeur and its concomitant Middle Eastern and Islamic culture is massively present, yet the long and sustained effort to excise it from the public mind has somehow left this heritage in the awkward position of touristic artefact.

This represents a problem for Turkish society in many ways, not least of which is the fact that Turkish nationalism remains strangely deficient. Movements for national pride and national independence typically go looking for an historical period where the nation in question can be shown to have proved its grandeur. In the Turkish case this golden age is overwhelmingly obviously that of the Seljuk and Ottoman Empires, yet for the Kemalist project in its heyday this heritage was virtually untouchable and

---

[8] Nereid, op. cit., p. 31.

they cast their eyes instead on the distant, half-mythical time of the Turkish nomads of Central Asia, which held much less of a place in the hearts of the people.[9]

## A Modern Islamic Alternative

Of course, in contrast to the sometimes rabid secularist and Westernising streak of the Kemalists, since the mid-nineteenth century there had existed alternative voices that were thoroughly in favour of modernisation, but that did not view Islam as inimical to progress. Members of the *Young Ottoman* movement like Namik Kemal, and later the Islamic reformists Jamal al-Din al-Afghani and Muhammad Abduh, saw in a reformed Islam an inspiration for a sustained development effort and at the same time a necessary bond of solidarity for Muslims to resist outside domination. In post-imperial Turkey the torch of an enlightened pro-modern Islam as a road to modernity and development was taken up by Said Nursi (1873-1960), a Sufi-trained Kurdish scholar from Eastern Anatolia. For Nursi, who had a burning wish to see his country develop and not least achieve a high level of modern education without losing its faith, Islam represented precisely 'an opening for the cultivation of rational thought and growth of modern scientific technology.'[10] The movement he founded, which came to be known as the *Nurcu*s, 'encouraged literacy, education and science as means to mobilise its members politically and thereby stimulated the development of a participant society.'[11] In a sense, and referring to the 'double loneliness' discussed above, the Nurcu movement can be seen as religion returning from below after its institutions and organisations have either been made subservient to the state or simply banned or swept away. It is extremely significant to note that, whether in Turkey or in other Muslim countries, this 'return from below' is hardly ever directed against modernisation as such. Actually those who take the initiative in forming movements of Islamic revival, whether these are explicitly political or not, are more often than not people who are benefiting from the modernising change taking place, in the form of social mobility through education or through exploitation of newly arising opportunities for business ventures. They typically aim, like Nursi, to help, not hinder, progressive development, but in doing so they want to reinstate religion as a moral framework for society. This combined orientation makes them

---

[9] For a treatment of Kemalist historiography, see Doğan Gürpınar, *The Seljuks of Rum in Turkish Republican Historiography* (Sabanci University, 2004).
[10] Atasoy, op. cit., p. 81.
[11] Nereid, op. cit., p. 46.

lean towards the need for a fresh interpretation of the religious sources, in order to make religion relevant to the issues of the day.[12]

In the case of the Nurcu they did not even challenge the principle of secularism or *laiklik* as such, merely the official interpretation of it. When multi-party politics emerged in Turkey after the Second World War, Said Nursi's followers threw their weight behind the oppositional Democratic Party (DP). In its 1946 programme the DP stated that it rejected 'the erroneous interpretation of secularism that has led to a hostile attitude towards religion' and advocated 'a clearer separation between religion and public affairs so that the government will not interfere in religious activities.'[13] The DP and the Nurcu, many of whom became active party members, chose to interpret *laiklik* as religious *freedom* from state interference, whereas the Republican People's Party (RPP), which remained in power until 1950, understood the same principle to mean the subordination and strict *control* of religion by the state.

In their ideas about progress and development, and about the need to advance rational and scientific thinking, the Nurcu were actually quite close to central aspects of Kemalist ideology. Yet throughout republican history both Said Nursi and his followers became subject (albeit to fluctuating degrees) to persecution and frequent arrests and internal displacements. The reason for this may of course be seen in their wanting to undertake modernisation under the banner of Islam, something that went clearly against what the Kemalists saw as sacred values of the Republic. Yet a couple of other reasons may be suggested as being of at least equal importance. One has to do with the fact that the Nurcu were harshly critical of nationalist ideology. As mentioned, Said Nursi himself was a Kurd. In 1925 he was accused of taking part in the Sait rebellion of that year (see above), although this was never proved. Nursi was against Kurdish as well as Turkish nationalism. Still his Kurdishness may have had something to do with his ideology. When Turkish nationalism became the dominant identity ideology of the new state, Nursi may have felt that this would make things worse for the Kurds than when in the Ottoman Empire they had been equal with their Turkish co-subjects vis-à-vis the legitimising principle of the state, Islam. Whatever the case, opposing nationalism in itself meant opposition to another of the basic principles of Kemalism. In the end the most disturbing thing about the Nurcu for the authorities was probably the fact that they represented an independent force gathering its resources directly from members of the public across Turkey. This kind of civil society raising its head with a focused strong loyalty to other than the

---

[12] Cf. Bjørn Olav Utvik, *The Pious Road to Development: Islamist Economics in Egypt* (London: Hurst, 2006), p. 26.
[13] Quoted here from Nereid, op. cit., p. 48.

head of state was something it would take many decades for the Turkish state to grow to (at least partly) accept.

## Religion in Multi-party Politics

When the DP won the elections in 1950 it ushered in a ten-year period under the rule of Prime Minister Adnan Menderes and President Celal Bayar, when the pressure on religious expression and organisation was somewhat lessened. The introduction of multi-party elections in 1946 had already induced the ruling RPP to take some steps to try to mend fences with religious voters. Thus from 1947 religion was again an optional subject in schools, and in 1949 a Faculty of Theology was opened in Ankara University. Once in power the DP went further. In a move of great symbolic significance the call to prayer again sounded in Arabic from 1950, religious instruction was expanded and there was a marked increase in the building of mosques. At the same time the persecution of religious activists was pursued with less vigour. The DP never renounced the principle of secularism, however, and though the conditions for independent religious life became less oppressive than before or after DP rule, a number of Nurcu members were still being arrested in the 1950s.

The DP government was toppled by a military coup in 1960, followed by the execution of Menderes and two other cabinet ministers. But as civilian politics returned the tendency of 'liberal Kemalism' represented by the DP, was re-elected to power for long periods in the last decades of the twentieth century, first in the shape of the Justice Party and (after the military banned all former parties in 1980) as the True Path Party, both led for a long time by former DP member Süleyman Demirel.

The more liberal attitude towards religion exhibited by the DP and its successors went some way towards appeasing resentment against the authoritarian secularising reforms of Atatürk. Yet with the gradual emergence of aspiring educational and business elites rooted in the provincial lower middle classes of Anatolian towns, the scene was set for the emergence of a more clear-cut Islamist political tendency. The first organisational expression of this in the form of a political party was the National Order Party established by the engineer Necmettin Erbakan in 1969. While this party was banned when the military took over in 1971, it re-emerged as the National Salvation Party (NSP), gathering about 10 per cent of the vote in the 1970s and taking part in several coalition governments. Like all other parties the NSP was banned in 1980 by the military government of General Evren, which held power till 1983. With his new Welfare Party, founded in 1983, Erbakan scored the greatest success of his career when the party emerged as the largest in the parliamentary election of 1995, leading to a coalition government headed by Erbakan in 1996-1997.

This government was forced out of office by the military in what has been described as a post-modern coup, and later the Welfare Party was banned for having violated the constitution's stipulations on secularism. Erbakan was now banned from taking part in politics for life. But the new Virtue Party picked up the torch despite a slight setback in elections in 1999. When even that party was banned, the Islamist movement split in two. A traditionalist wing, led by Erbakan loyalist Recai Kutan formed the Felicity Party [*Saadat Partisi*], while the modernist wing under former Istanbul Mayor Recep Teyyip Erdogan established the Party of Justice and Development, better known under its Turkish acronym AKP [*Adalet ve Kalkinma Partisi*]. While the traditionalists were reduced to insignificance in the elections of November 2002, the AKP swept to victory. With the support of 34 per cent of the voters, due to the peculiarities of the Turkish electoral system they gained 66 per cent of the seats in Parliament and have headed the government since.

Many Turkish Islamists including the current AKP leadership have been in close contact with the mainstream Arab Islamist movement, the Muslim Brotherhood (MB). But unlike the MB and other Islamist movements in the Arab world the religious parties in Turkey never demanded the introduction of an Islamic state ruled by the Sharia. Of course this must be seen against the background of Turkish law, jealously guarded by the powerful military, which makes it illegal to put forward such demands in Turkey. Thus, despite the fact that at least some tendencies within the parties saw the introduction of Sharia as a long-term goal, in order to make use of the legal political space in Turkey they had to refrain from saying so in public.

Yet beyond that it is probably fair to say that the Islamic parties in Turkey have broadly speaking not seen it as their task to impose religious restrictions on the public, but rather to remove public restrictions on religious life. It would seem that, while emphasising the need for religion to provide moral guidance for society and politics, they have more or less adhered to the liberal interpretation of the secularist character of the state, referred to above in connection with the DP. In the case of the AKP, seen by many as the expression of a *post*-Islamist tendency, virtually all explicit reference to religion has been dropped from the party programme.[14] Yet alongside its modernist and pro-European stance, the party strives to strengthen the hold of (sometimes quite traditional) morality in society, and to remove restrictions of religious expression like the ban on headscarves for women generally enforced in public institutions, most notably in schools and universities.

In an interesting parallel to developments in many Arab countries, in the 1980s important elements in the Kemalist establishment and its military core saw it as

---

[14] English Translation of the AKP Programme, http://www.cesnur.org/2004/akp.htm.

prudent to put more emphasis on religion in their own rhetoric. This 'Islamisation-from-above' policy was partly aimed at containing leftist elements, partly at taking the ground from under the Islamists, as it were; in a recognition of the population's strong attachment to Islam and Islamic ideals it was felt necessary to link regime legitimacy to the faith by symbolic moves that would be welcomed by the pious masses. In Turkey this took the form of regime espousal of the so-called Turco-Islamic synthesis. After the military coup of 1980, both the military leadership of General Kenan Evren (who remained President of the Republic until 1989) and its civilian successor the Motherland Party led by Turgut Özal, promoted this synthesis as the proper legitimising ideology of the Turkish state.[15]

Though taking up the themes in a century-old debate about the relation between nationalism and religion, in its current form the Turco-Islamic synthesis was put forth by Ibrahim Kafesoglu, leading ideologue of the *Aydinlar Ocagi* [Hearths of the Enlightened], a group formed in 1970 to counter what was seen as a left-wing hegemony in ideological and cultural debate in the country. The basic idea was that the Turks were strongly attached to Islam because it resonated with central elements of their own pre-Islamic culture: 'a deep sense of justice, monotheism and a belief in the immortal soul, and a strong emphasis on family life and morality.'[16] The Turks held a special mission as the soldiers of Islam. Turkish culture, then, was built on two pillars: 'a 2,500-year-old Turkish element and a 1,000-year-old Islamic element.'[17] In accordance with this the military government also for the first time since the twenties made 'religion and ethics' a compulsory part of the basic curriculum in all schools.

Concurrent with these developments was the gradual emergence of a distinct nostalgia for the Ottoman Empire, or what became known as 'Neo-Ottomanism', expressed both in an increased interest in the historical heritage and in a new foreign policy propounded by Turgut Özal where he broke with Kemalist isolationism in favour of an active interest in developments in the Balkans, the Caucasus, Central Asia and the Middle East.[18]

In this atmosphere, of course, it was also easier for the Islamists to breathe, once they had reorganised themselves after the initial suppression following the coup, and we have seen the successes they came to achieve. From one perspective what happened can be seen as the gradual emergence of the 'common people' of Turkish, and in particular Anatolian society into the public realm, hitherto dominated by the

---

[15] Atasoy, op. cit., p. 153.
[16] Zürcher, op. cit., p. 303.
[17] ibid.
[18] Sedat Laciner, 'Özalism (Neo-Ottomanism): An Alternative in Turkish Foreign Policy?', *Journal of Administrative Sciences*, vol. 1, nos. 1-2, (2003-2004), pp. 175 ff.

Kemalist elite. Through long-term processes of mobilisation linked to economic development, improved communication and not least expanded access to education, the common people became visible, as it were. And these were deeply religious people. According to a survey carried out as recently as 2000, as many as 46 per cent pray five times a day, 84 per cent of men go to communal prayers in the mosque each Friday, 91 per cent fast during Ramadan, 60 per cent give the prescribed religious alms, the *zakat*, and 71 per cent would go on the pilgrimage to Mecca, the *hajj*, if they could. As broader layers of this population were drawn into public life, they did not (in the words of a writer describing the same process in nineteenth-century Norway) 'accept to remain quiet' and when they spoke, it was, to the astonishment of the established elites, in order to demand 'public space for an outdated piety.'[19]

## Return to the Past or to the Future?

But a closer analysis would show that what was involved in the renewed prominence of a religious discourse was not the return of the old religion; rather it was a question of religious people negotiating their road to modernity from within tradition. As I have argued elsewhere the Islamist movement in general carries many modernising traits. It contributes to an individualisation of responsibility, it mobilises for social and political engagement of new sectors of the population from outside the established elites, it has a persistent focus on the furthering of economic development, and it fights tirelessly against corruption and in favour of substituting a meritocratic system in economic, organisational and political life for the currently dominant clientel structures.[20]

In the Turkish case the series of parties led by Necmettin Erbakan from the seventies through the nineties exhibit these same features, albeit drawing more heavily on traditional patron-client patterns, hierarchical bonds of loyalty and protection known as *himaye*, in building their networks across society. Among the 'generation of the seventies' who gradually came to dominate mainstream Islamist activism in the country, and who went on to form the current ruling party, the AKP, the modernising traits are much more clear-cut. Though this generation is still apt at mobilising

---

[19] Arne Bugge Amundsen, 'Konventikler og vekkelser', in A.B. Amundsen (ed.), *Norges religionshistorie* (Oslo: Universitetsforlaget, 2005), p. 312.
[20] Cf. Bjørn Olav Utvik, 'The modernizing force of Islamism', in François Burgat and John Esposito (eds.), *Modernizing Islam: Religion and the Public Sphere in the Middle East and Europe* (London: Hurst / Piscataway, NJ: Rutgers University Press, 2003).

through family structures, focus is now much more on horizontal ties of communal solidarity and mutual help, what is traditionally known as *imece*.[21]

As seen above on the question of Islamic legislation, the Turkish Islamists come out as more liberal than their Arab counterparts, preferring to speak of greater tolerance and freedom of religious expression, rather than to seek the imposition of Islamic norms on all. They do not challenge the secular nature of the Turkish state, but propose a contending vision of what secularism is about. In this sense, they do, in the tradition of the DP, represent a break with the authoritarian social engineering from above of what has been termed High Kemalism,[22] in that they reintroduce the common people as legitimate subjects of the polity, as these common people are.

In the case of the now-dominant AKP they explicitly support the secular nature of the state, but insist that this is a principle that demands that the state be active in enforcing religious freedom. Otherwise the AKP programme, while heavily concentrated on economic and administrative development, gives central emphasis to the promotion of human rights, democracy, freedom of expression, the elimination of corruption and calls for a state based on law. Significantly it insists that this last point presupposes that all laws are based on universally accepted principles of respect for human rights, equality of all citizens, and the protections of the rights and freedoms of the individual.[23] And interestingly the list is remarkably parallel to the list of demands of the reformist movement in the Islamic Republic of Iran, which itself is struggling to reform an authoritarian republic where authoritarianism has been legitimised with reference to religion. In both cases the resultant de-ideologised reform calls could be considered as so detached from religious ideology that they warrant the label of post-Islamism. Yet it is equally clear in both cases that the movements in question are definitely the legitimate children of an Islamist environment.

## An Islamic Road to Europe?

Whatever the case, it would seem that the movement represented today by the AKP, in its refocusing on pride in the historical heritage of Turkish society in Eastern Thrace and Anatolia, is not primarily concerned with a return to the past. Perhaps we should see it rather as a return to the present and the future. The AKP sees coming to terms with tradition, and with the events and cultural traits that have formed today's Turks, as an advantage rather than something blocking progress. It could be argued that it

---

[21] Jenny B. White, *Islamist Mobilization in Turkey: A Study in Vernacular Politics* (Seattle: University of Washington Press, 2002), pp. 69 ff.
[22] Cagaptay, op. cit., p. 43.
[23] English Translation of the AKP Programme, http://www.cesnur.org/2004/akp.htm.

thus provides the country and its inhabitants with the confidence to deal more squarely with the issues facing them today. In this sense it is perhaps no accident that the AKP government has moved more rapidly forward *both* in developing ties with neighbouring, mostly Muslim, countries to the east and south, *and* in strengthening human rights and democracy and preparing the way for Turkish entry to the European Union.

In opposition to what has been the ruling discourse throughout Turkey's republican history, the AKP insists that building a modern state ruled by a law, which protects the freedom of the individual as well as the common good, does not require a break with Islam, but is rather the realisation of a true understanding of this religion. It aspires to Turkish membership of the European family as a moderate nation of Muslims sharing basic values with the Christian-majority countries. It looks upon itself as a Muslim version of the Christian-democratic parties of Europe and is seeking to build party-to-party contacts on that basis.[24]

In a sense the party advocates moving into partnership with European countries on the basis of a modernity anchored in a reformed and updated understanding of one's own culture and history. Incidentally, this would seem a far more rational and scientific approach than the favoured Kemalist idea, formed in a desperate attempt to fill the void left by the break with real history, and forced on Turkish pupils through the decades, that Turks were the ones who established all the great human civilisations and that Turkish was the mother of all languages.[25]

Despite the hesitation expressed by certain sections of European societies and political elites, especially since the start of the 'war on terror', about the thought of having a populous Muslim-majority country entering the European club, the rise of the Islamist tendency may thus eventually turn out to have cleared the road for greater Turkish integration into the European family. In a sense what is happening could be seen as Turkey absorbing itself, as it were, in the process confronting the bulk of the population and the religion they adhere to directly with the problems of modernity and of relating to the outside world. This would prepare the ground for a much more thoroughgoing reform than what could be achieved with force from above.

This would definitely be in line with the optimistic view of former Prime Minister and President Turgut Özal, who incidentally had a past in the Islamist movement, running as a candidate for the National Salvation Party for Izmir in the parliamentary elections of 1979. Contrary to the belief of the earlier Kemalists that anything reminiscent of the Ottoman-Islamic past must be eradicated for Turkey to take the

---

[24] Breffni O'Rourke, 'Turkey: AKP Tries to Join European Conservative Group', http://www.eurasianet.org/departments/insight/articles/eav040603.shtml.
[25] Cagaptay, op. cit., pp. 50-51.

Western road to progress, Özal considered that Turkey's Ottoman heritage was its most important advantage in entering the Western club.[26]

---

[26] Sedat Laciner, 'Özalism (Neo-Ottomanism): An Alternative in Turkish Foreign Policy?', *Journal of Administrative Sciences*, vol. 1, nos 1-2, (2003-2004), p. 171.

# Turkey's Ambiguous Identity: The Symbolic Significance of EU Membership

Pınar Tank

## Introduction[1]

An image often used to represent Turkey is that of a bridge linking two continents, Europe and Asia, a country with a secure foothold on both sides of the divide. Turkish policymakers promote the image, emphasising Turkey's utility to the West as a 'go-between' to the East, a cultural interpreter of sorts. Reinforcing this idea is the historical trajectory of the state whose past is in the East yet whose future is sought in the West.

External perceptions of Turkey's geographical location aid in the formation of the country's identity; to a significant degree, Turkey's sense of self relies on the mirror held up to it by the outside world. Turkish policymakers reinforce this image using foreign policy as a tool in the construction of identity. This process, in turn has domestic implications for perceptions of national identity. In short, the construction of Turkey's identity as Western and secular emerges from the interplay between internal (national) and external (international) perceptions. Peter van Ham explains the development of state identity by applying the strategy of 'branding' as used in the business world. He notes that while a 'brand is described as a customer's idea about a product; the 'brand state' comprises the outside world's ideas about a particular country' (van Ham 2001, p. 2). Manipulating its history, geography and culture, the brand state constructs an identity, a unique image, which may fill a particular 'niche' in the geopolitical space.

---

[1] This chapter is an earlier version of an article entitled 'Dressing for the Occasion: Reconstructing Turkey's Identity?', *Journal of Southeast European and Black Sea Studies*, vol. 6, no. 4 (London: Taylor & Francis, December 2006), pp. 463-479.

The idea that identities are 'chosen' rather than 'given' challenges the notion of identity fixed by geopolitical criteria and ascribes a more active role to the state in defining identity. In the traditional study of geopolitics, there is an explicit focus on geography (in its purest form the study of land masses and seas) that assumes that where a state is physically in the world affects the limits and opportunities of political action.[2] This implies that state identity has a static nature, predetermined by geographical constraints. However, even traditional geopolitics includes elements of culture.[3] And, of equal importance to the geographic space a state occupies, is the fluid 'imaginative space' it inhabits, often perceived through its culture.

The issue of culture as it refers to identity has been the source of heated debate in Turkey. As in France, the 'headscarf issue' has become an example of the power of cultural/religious symbols in the struggle over national identity.[4] The ambiguity surrounding Turkey's identity is commonly attributed to the internal tension between the modern secular state with its ideological commitment to Westernisation and the traditional Muslim roots of the country. In the cultural context of the Middle East, Turkey lies in a grey area, a secular republic built on Western foundations out of the ashes of the multi-cultural Ottoman Empire. Huntington aptly labels Turkey a 'torn country' due to the ambiguity of its identity (Huntington 1996, p. 74).

However, for the political and military elite who set their sights on Turkey's inclusion in Western civilisation from the outset of the Turkish Republic, the country's identity is non-negotiable. Once again, using van Ham's analogy of branding, it is clear that the Turkish elite have sought to strengthen the state's Western identity through the development of a good 'brand' which affects not only how the outside world perceives the state but also the self-perception of the people within the state. In other words, 'branding' has also been utilised to strengthen Turkish national identity as secular and Western. Security concerns following the Second World War served to reinforce the logic sustaining Turkey's efforts to anchor itself solidly in the West. A corollary of this effort has been the repression of Turkey's Muslim identity despite the deeply religious sentiments of its traditional classes. More recently, however, the popularity of the moderate Islamic Justice and Development Party (AKP) government has raised questions about the officially Western identity of the Turkish

---

[2] Daniel Deudney makes the point that the term 'geopolitics' is often vaguely defined and overused. In an effort to clarify the term, he offers five distinct ideas that define the study of geopolitics. In the Turkish case, the most befitting understanding would be 'realism with an emphasis on geographical factors', see Deudney (1997), pp. 91-123.

[3] Guzzini makes the point that even MacKinder's writings on the dichotomy of sea and land powers were informed by cultural stereotypes, see Guzzini (2003), p. 6.

[4] For more on the struggle between the state and society over secularity, see Tank (2005).

Republic. The AKP represents an alternative 'brand' through which Turkey embodies a progressive, democratic, Muslim state. For the Turkish military, which has historically defined the state's Western trajectory, an ambiguous identity brings with it the perils of cultural uncertainty.

This sense of uncertainty is exacerbated by academics writing about Turkey after September 11th, who have often noted the country's potential as a 'model' for the Muslim world (Fuller 2002, pp. 48-60; Taspınar 2003). They have also pointed to the problems inherent in making this claim, indicating that the Turkish case might be *sui generis*, a model that emerges out of an overlap of particular cultural, social and historical circumstances (Taspınar 2003, p. v). While it may be the case that the Turkish model arises from a unique set of conditions, an examination of the 'Muslim model' claim made by scholars and policymakers is interesting in that it illustrates the objectives that may be attained through manipulating the country's selective identity.

This essay examines the country's ambiguous identity through the lens of critical geopolitics and in relation to the question of EU membership seeking to illustrate the symbolic significance of EU membership for the secular elite, and in particular for the Turkish Armed Forces.

## Westernisation Adopted under Pressure

The Turkish Armed Forces have been at the forefront of the Westernisation effort in Turkey since the eighteenth century, guiding the nation towards the ideological goal of Westernisation while guarding against any deviation from the Westernising project. Already from the end of the 1800s, emphasis was placed on the need to adopt Western 'civilisation' as a whole on the path to both material and cultural progress (Berkes 1964, p. 296). It was considered the highest form of culture and society to which Turkey should aspire. However, despite the modern Republic's admiration for all things Western, the process of Westernisation, adopted during the Ottoman period, arose out of necessity rather than design. The Ottomans begrudgingly implemented Western reforms in an effort to salvage the Empire following military defeats from the seventeenth century onwards and it was the decline of the Ottoman Empire that led Turkey down the path of Westernisation.

Turkey's Westernisation process was launched as a defensive response, illustrated by the following historical losses. The first were the Ottoman defeats of the late seventeenth century which forced a process of self-examination. The failure of the second siege of Vienna in 1683, followed by the overthrow of Ottoman power in Hungary and the loss of Buda three years later, weakened the Empire and led to the peace treaty signed at Karlowitz between the Ottoman Empire and the Holy League in

1699.[5] The Ottomans were humiliated by the territorial losses sustained at the hands of a superior military force and as a consequence the treaty had a significant effect on Ottoman regard for the Christian world in which they had been disinterested up to that point. Although their defeat was originally attributed to military decline, in time the Ottomans recognised that their losses were, in fact, equally due to the economic and technological innovations of the nascent nation states of Western Europe (Zürcher 1993, p. 21). The Treaty of Karlowitz also ushered in a new Ottoman understanding of the conduct of diplomacy as the Ottomans were forced to negotiate in order to alleviate their losses, and accept the equality of their adversaries.[6]

The recognition of European supremacy in military matters was a catalyst for the gradual process of modernisation in the Ottoman Empire. Military defeats by Russia from 1768 to 1774 led to the Treaty of Küçük Kaynarca through which Russia obtained rights of navigation through the straits, raising the threat of a Russian conquest of Istanbul. A final blow was the loss of the Crimea to Russia. This unprecedented defeat, Muslim territory lost to a Christian power, further reinforced the argument for modernisation by adopting the ways of the infidel.

The reform process continued through the eighteenth and nineteenth centuries, although it faced resistance from sectors of Ottoman society. In particular the janissaries, the infantry of the Ottoman army, feared the loss of their power.[7] A second important phase in the Westernisation process began in the nineteenth century, and was referred to as the *Tanzimat* (1839-1871). The centralising and modernising reforms of the Tanzimat period sought to strengthen the state both from external attack and internal disintegration through importing the military, administrative and educational institutions of the West (Hale 1994, p. 13). As such, Tanzimat reforms were a result of external pressures and aimed to either gain foreign support for the

---

[5] The Holy League was a coalition of various European powers including Austria-Hungary, Poland, Venice and Russia formed between 1510 and 1511 in order to defend the states of Italy against Louis XII of France and thereby strengthen the power of the pope. The Treaty of Karlowitz, brought to an end the Austro-Ottoman war (1683-1697) and the westward expansion of the Ottoman Empire.

[6] Previous peace treaties signed by the Ottomans had been dictated on the Empire's own terms and accepted by the defeated party. As a result, the Treaty of Karlowitz was the first negotiated peace treaty signed by a defeated Ottoman Empire against superior Christian adversaries (Zürcher 1993, p. 18).

[7] Sultan Selim's 'new order', *Nizam-I Cedid*, (1789-1807) was a threat to the established power of the janissaries. Selim decreed the creation a new corps of infantry and artillery based on the European model with modern weapons and European expertise. The janissaries were eventually defeated in 1826 (Hale 1994, p. 15).

Ottoman Empire's efforts at maintaining control over its territory or at the least prevent foreign intervention in the affairs of the Empire (Zürcher 1993, p. 53).[8]

The period of the Tanzimat was a transition between the end of the traditional order and the formation of the Turkish republic in 1923, the third significant advance towards the West. Mustafa Kemal Atatürk, the military leader and founder of modern Turkey, was an ardent believer in Turkey's place in the West. However, among the nationalists, there were those who felt that Western ideas had to be carefully balanced against national culture. Most important among them was Ziya Gökalp, the ideologue of Turkish nationalism who developed a political-social theory of 'Turkish-Islamist-Westernist Modernism'. He expressed the social ideal that formed the basis of Turkish nationalism: 'We are of the Turkish nation [*millet*] of the Islamic religious community [*ümmet*], of Western civilisation [*medeniyet*]' (Parla 1985, p. 25). Gökalp made a distinction between 'culture' which referred to subjective, relative national characteristics and 'civilisation' which comprised the realm of objective, scientific reason. Turkish nationalism, based on Islamic religion, formed the cultural basis for social solidarity while 'judgements of facts and their science fall essentially in the domain of civilisation which is international' (p. 28). In this manner, he attempted to preserve national culture based on Islamic civilisation while adopting the 'reason and science and technology of contemporary (sic: Western) civilization' (p. 29). Gökalp maintained that Tanzimat modernism had failed because it had rejected Islam, focusing instead on multi-religious Ottomanism favouring what he referred to as 'cosmopolitanism', an uncritical acceptance of Western culture at the expense of traditional values.

However, Gökalp's subtle distinctions between culture and civilisation did not prevail; the Kemalists ardently adopted Western civilisation and culture as the foundations of modern Turkish identity. The conviction with which Westernisation was embraced was expressed in 1913 by Abdullah Cevdet, a Young Turk author: 'There is no second civilization; civilization means European civilization, and it must be imported with both its roses and its thorns' (Lewis 1968, p. 236). The positivist view of civilisation held by the Kemalist reformers necessitated secularisation first, followed by modernisation. The abolition of the sultanate and caliphate and replacement of the old legal system with the Swiss civil and Italian penal codes removed Islamic legal precepts from the judicial system. The challenge was not simply to secularise the state in the modernisation process but additionally to 'civilise' the

---

[8] From European powers, there was pressure for improvements in the position of Christian minority communities within the Empire who were regarded as second-class subjects. The Gülhane edict of 1839 officially elevated their status to that of the Muslim majority. In part the Gülhane edict was a diplomatic manoeuvre to gain British support for the Ottoman Empire's struggle against the Egyptian army. It was, however, an important reform document as it addressed the rights of citizens for the first time.

new Turkish citizen. The military were designated by Atatürk as both the vanguard of the revolution and the guardian of its secular values. The Kemalist cultural revolution, in essence a social engineering project, replaced both social structures and cultural symbols with adopted Western substitutes. This comprised a wide spectrum of changes: secular Western instead of Islamic education, European law in place of Islamic jurisprudence, the Latin instead of Arabic alphabet, women's rights, Western dress styles, the Gregorian calendar and classical music (Rustow 1988, p. 244).

The longing to be a part of the West, initially brought on by failure in the military sphere, over time translated into a sense of inferiority in the cultural arena. The Islamic past was disparaged as an impediment towards progress, and efforts continue to this day to suppress symbols of Turkey's Muslim identity in the fear that they may destroy the achievements of the secular state. Kemalism's militant secularism created what political scientist Binnaz Toprak eloquently phrased, 'a nation of forgetters' (Toprak 1981, p. 47). The rise of the AKP, however, begs the question: 'Can Turkey's "forgotten" Islamic identity prove instrumental in its relationship with the West?'

## Defining Moments in Turkey's Relations with the West

Turkey's desire to be included in the West was based on an ideological commitment to Western civilisation. However, this commitment alone does not explain Turkey's Westernisation project. Equally important were the country's security needs; these reinforced the bond to the West interlocking the state's cultural and security identities.[9] The need to secure Turkey throughout the Cold War period and the state elite's acknowledgement that this was best achieved through strengthening the bond with the United States and Europe bolstered Turkey's cultural trajectory.

There have been several 'defining moments' in the relationship in which the state, through foreign policy decisions, underlined its commitment to the West. Reaffirmation from the West of Turkey's value has served in turn to strengthen the bond. What follows is a brief overview of critical moments in modern Turkey's courtship of the West in which one can observe the changing nature of the commitment in line with U.S. and European needs.

Joining NATO in 1952 indicated Turkey's acceptance into a cultural as well as a defensive alliance. As Kamran Inan, a former ambassador and member of the Turkish national assembly wrote in 1974, 'Our membership in NATO is, first of

---

[9] In fact, during the 1923-1946 single-party period when Turkey's secularisation and Westernisation policies were at their height, there was no noteworthy effort to build an exclusive relationship to the West. On the contrary, relations with Russia were good and Turkey sought regional defence and non-aggression pacts, such as the Saadabad, an unsuccessful effort to forge a pact with Iran and Afghanistan.

all, an important stride in our westernisation movement. We have obtained a place and a say within the Atlantic community. The frontiers of Europe now begin from Eastern Turkey.'[10] Nonetheless, while NATO purported to be a 'community based on common values', strategic considerations were as important in assessing Turkey's application as value-based arguments.

Despite finally achieving membership, Turkey's initial efforts were rebuffed. At the time, NATO lacked a broad strategy towards the region due to the Eastern Mediterranean being seen as on the periphery of European security concerns (Kaplan and Clawson 1985). The inclusion of both Turkey and Greece in NATO was opposed by several of the founding members. The British government felt that a separate Middle East defence alliance should be established around Turkey and Greece rather than admitting them as NATO members. The Nordic countries, for their part, were concerned that the inclusion of Turkey and Greece would prove an over-extension of the NATO sphere.

In the end, the policies of the United States determined the Alliance's policy in the Eastern Mediterranean region. The United States became aware of the strategic importance of Turkey in containing the Soviet expansionist threat as early as 1945. Demands by the Soviet Union for greater involvement in governing the Turkish straits as well as claims to parts of Eastern Anatolia in 1945 brought attention to Turkey's potential role in the American policy of containment. As such, Turkey (along with Iran) was one of the first countries to become party to the regional rivalry between the United States and the Soviet Union (Cleveland 1994). Turkey, for its part, backed up its commitment to the West with military force. A month after the Korean War broke out in 1950, it committed 4,500 troops to the UN forces making it the second largest foreign military engaged in Korea after the United States. While Turkey's entry into the organisation was undoubtedly based on the geo-strategic needs of the Cold War, membership made Turkey part of the alliance's civilisational community, thus reinforcing Turkey's cultural identity through its security role. Turkey was heralded by the United States as a symbol of a secular, democratic state, a rarity in the regional context. Both the process and the rationale whereby Turkey attained NATO membership would have an impact on future negotiations with the European Union in which the Turkish elite often argued for inclusion based on strategic factors rather than the fulfilment of European norms and standards.

However, Turkey's pro-Western foreign policy during the Cold War came at a cost. The country's single-minded Westernisation at the expense of good relations in the Middle East fuelled perceptions in the Arab world that it served as a lackey of

---

[10] Cited in Yılmaz and Bilgin 2005, p. 52.

the United States. These charges built on Turkey's historical affinity with the West and lack of solidarity with the Middle East. For example, in the period of pan-Arab nationalism Turkey chose to ignore the aspirations of its Middle Eastern neighbours and in so doing damaged its regional relations. Ömer Taspınar notes that Turkey was the first Muslim state to recognise Israel and it voted with France against Algeria in the UN at the time of the Algerian War of Independence. Relations with Syria were strained after the 1939 dispute over Alexandrette (Hatay) while those with Nasser's Egypt were affected by Turkey's recognition of Israel (Taspınar 2003, p. 10). Nor was there much support from the Arab world toward Turkey's policies: none of the Arab states recognised the Turkish Republic of Northern Cyprus after it declared independence in 1983 and they systematically voted against Turkey on the issue at the United Nations. Throughout the Cold War, Turkey maintained the traditional Kemalist line towards the Arab world, choosing to remain distant and disengaged.

While turning its back on the East, Turkey sought to reinforce its ties with the West through closer integration with Europe. In 1963, Turkey signed an Association Agreement with the then European Economic Community. The agreement granted Turkey a 'European vocation' and affirmed its right to accede to the European Community (Vaner 2003). Nonetheless subsequent applications by Turkey to the EEC and later the EU, were rejected first on the basis of economic criteria and later, increasingly, on the basis of normative criteria. The decision in 1995 to sign a trade agreement with Ankara raised hopes of full membership but these were crushed at the Luxembourg summit of 1997 after which an angry Turkey became less amenable towards the EU. The impasse in relations was not broken until the 1999 decision of the EU to extend membership candidacy to Turkey upon fulfilment of the Copenhagen criteria. However, the long struggle with the EU and the organisation's reticence to include Turkey left its mark: the secular elite in particular were suspicious of the EU's requirements for membership as set out in the Copenhagen criteria preferring instead to maintain closer relations with the United States so as to anchor Turkey in the West.

Meanwhile other developments following the end of the Cold War encouraged Turkish policymakers to take a more active role in the Middle East. There was speculation initially that Turkey's strategic importance to NATO would decline, reducing its value as a Western ally, due to the diminished threat from the Soviet Union. However, Turkey was soon given the opportunity to prove its continuing importance to the West: Turkey's decision to join the Gulf War in 1990-1991, while placing the country strategically within the context of the Middle East and the Gulf region, also reaffirmed its commitment to the West (Sezer 1996, p. 77). The decision to take part in the Gulf War coalition was in large part due to the opportunity recognised by President Türgüt Özal for emphasising Turkey's continuing strategic significance. It was, however, deeply unpopular with the Turkish General Staff whose attitude to the crisis indicated its more traditional view of Turkey's non-interventionist role in the Middle East and ultimately resulted in the resignations of the Chief of Staff Torumtay as well as the defence and foreign ministers (Larrabee and Lesser 2003, p. 134).

After the Gulf War, increased awareness of the plight of the Kurds (spread across Turkey, Iraq, Syria and Iran) and the worsening of Turkey's relations with its own Kurdish minority drew the country into regional politics. Cross border 'hot pursuit' operations against PKK rebels in Iraq indicated the extent to which the non-interventionist attitude had changed. These also served to reinforce the credibility of Turkish threats of intervention across other regional boundaries in the interests of Turkish internal security. Academics such as Huntington further reinforced the perception of Turkey's turn eastward, contending that the rise of global divisions based on religious and ethnic differences after the end of the Cold War repositioned Turkey in the Middle East (Huntington 1993, pp. 22-49). Although Turkey's shifting geopolitical position may have placed it further East, and raised internal concerns about the country's strategic relevance to the West, the Gulf War had illustrated that the shift to the East made the country all the more important as a Western ally. Further reinforcing Turkey's Western identity was the country's 1996 military agreement with Israel which both strengthened ties with the United States and allowed access to the influential Jewish lobby in Washington.

While the relationship with Israel brought Turkey closer to the United States, the improvement of relations between Ankara and Tehran from the mid-1990s was more in line with the European policy of constructive engagement (Larrabee and Lesser 2003, p. 148). In sum, developments after the Gulf War advanced Turkey's value as a regional actor with a Western, secular identity. However, events since 9/11, and particularly after the Iraq War, have created a new interest among Turkish policymakers in promoting the country's Muslim identity.

## Turkish Identity post-9/11 from a Critical Geopolitics Framework

As shown above, Turkey has historically sought to emphasise its Western over its Eastern identity. Although policymakers popularly like to express the idea of the country as a bridge between East and West, this has been a formulation intended to highlight Turkey's value to the West, rather than paying homage to its intrinsic 'Easternness'. Critical geopolitics provides a valuable framework for understanding how Turkey's identity is made use of through geographical discourse to serve political purposes. Originating from political geography and influenced by the constructionist approach, critical geopolitics aims to uncover the strategic importance and manipulative power of geopolitical representations. In a Derridean manner, 'critical geopolitics involves deconstructing the ways in which political elites have depicted and represented places in their exercise of power' and in so doing, it seeks to expose the symbolic, hidden power of the geographical discourse (Reuber 2000, p. 38). By applying critical geopolitics to the Turkish case, one can explain the secular elite's power derived from a definition of the country's identity as exclusively Western.

Critical geopolitics is also a particularly useful tool in the analysis of international relations after the end of the Cold War when the definition of security has widened to include the politics of identity. In the case of Turkey, the importance of 'fixing' its identity is key at a time when culture is 'securitised' through the war on terror with its civilisational leitmotif. Wæver explains that in traditional concepts of security the referent object of security is the 'state' and not the 'nation'. However, with the end of the Cold War and the growth of identity based conflicts, it is the survival of the nation, through the preservation of its societal identity inscribed in its 'culture' and 'values' that is the focus of security. When the political elite chooses to define a threat to the nation's existence in identity terms, it becomes a 'societal security issue' (Wæver 2000, p. 29). Through this process of naming threats to identity (and by extension, to the 'nation'), culture becomes securitised. In Turkey, two dominant identities, the 'secular nation' and 'Islamist nation' vie against one another within the Kemalist state. The discussion of culture/identity in security terms increases the perception of threat when accepted versions of identity are challenged. Societal security implies that a society persist *in its essential character* under changing conditions' (Wæver, Buzan, Kelstrup and Lemaitre 1993, p. 23). Therefore, it is disconcerting for the secular elite in Turkey that references to the country's identity as 'Western and secular' are increasingly being replaced with those of 'Muslim and democratic'. However, Bill McSweeney argues that societal identity, instead of being an objective, static, reality to be analysed and discovered as Wæver assumes, is rather a 'process of negotiation among people and interest groups...'[11] The debate over Turkey's identity may prove a case in point.

## Interlocking of the 'Civilisational' and Security Arguments

In the aftermath of 9/11 and the Iraq War, Turkey has sought to promote itself as a model state in which Islam and democracy coexist. This has been a particularly

---

[11] McSweeney is critical of Wæver for presenting a near-positivist conception of identity (McSweeney 1999, pp. 68-79).

useful policy vis-à-vis the United States which in late 2003, announced the 'Middle East Partnership Initiative', proposing swift democratisation for the states of the Middle East as an offensive in the war on terror. In the months that followed, this policy was modified somewhat in response to criticisms that democracy cannot be imposed. Thus, the G8 Summit in June 2004 reformulated the 'democracy initiative' as a 'democracy dialogue' with the Middle East and renamed it the Broader Middle East and North Africa Initiative (BME Initiative). In line with this thinking, Turkish policymakers reformulated Turkey's role to that of assisting and supporting the 'dialogue' project and publicly rejected the idea of a Turkish 'model'. In Turkish Foreign Minister Gül's words, Turkey was the 'perfect embodiment of modernity, progress, identity and tradition' with a unique position from which to 'facilitate interaction and dialogue between the Islamic World and the West' (Gül 2004). This discourse, more acceptable to Arab and North African states, did not, however, diminish the fact that the Turkish political elite aspired to the 'model' role.

Despite the criticism of U.S. policy in the Middle East, the discourse of reform and democratisation became a part of regional discussions. This was evident at the June 2004 Organisation of the Islamic Conference meeting where Iraq and democratic reform dominated discussions. Turkish President Ahmet Necdet Sezer concluded that Muslim leaders had to accept that change and determine its shape for themselves before being pressured into it (Meixler 2004). The challenge is to adopt democratic reforms within the context of the local culture without imposing Western values. As such, Turkish policymakers promoted the country's unique position as a secular state governed by a moderate Muslim party actively seeking democratic reforms. The Turkish military's acceptance of the AKP's strategy, albeit sceptical, lends credibility to the model indicating the possibility of a successful marriage between secular state and Islamic traditions.

The search for a model of Islam that represents both moderation and democratic values has provided the AKP with a unique opportunity to position itself vis-à-vis the traditionally secular political elite. In doing so, it has pursued an activist foreign policy. This has been most evident in the assertive approach taken towards the European Union where it has pursued an alternative 'branding' of Turkey. In a turnaround of Turkish policy towards the EU in December 2002, then Prime Minister Gül and party leader Erdogan argued at the Copenhagen Summit for the inclusion of Turkey based on its Muslim identity. This was a sharp departure from the past when Turkish policymakers, through consecutive efforts at membership, had based membership applications on the country's scrupulously crafted, and painstakingly guarded, Western identity. The focus on the country's Western identity can be attributed to the sense in Turkey that the EU's rejection of its many applications was based primarily on religious factors. As an example, in 1997, despite Turkey's inability to meet EU requirements on human rights, the Cyprus problem and the Kurdish issue, former Turkish Prime Minister Bülent Ecevit maintained that: 'The real reason is that they don't want a Muslim country in their midst' (*The Economist*, 24 April 1999). For the secular elite for whom the modern Republic is unquestionably Western, the EU's rejection of Turkey based on cultural criteria was a bitter pill to swallow.

Undoubtedly, the historical representation of Turks in the West plays a significant role in European perceptions of Turkey's identity. The EU's policies until recently endorsed a narrow definition of Europe in which Turks continued to symbolise the 'barbarian Other' stopped at the gates of Vienna, a reference to the expansionary efforts of the Ottoman Empire. However, as Uffe Østergaard notes, the Ottoman Empire in 1910 was comprised of four religions and 41 per cent of its population was in fact Orthodox Christian.[12] Although the secular republic founded by Atatürk broke dramatically with the past rejecting the Ottoman heritage, Turkey's present civilisational status remains a captive to the symbolic power of its historical roots. Furthermore, the secular Kemalist state has struggled for its place in Europe only to be found wanting where European democratic norms and standards are concerned.

If Turkey's identity is a captive to its historical roots, then the European Union is equally so. Norman Davies explains the origins of the European idea in historical terms; 'Europe' as a concept is a relatively modern idea evolving from the fourteenth to the eighteenth centuries replacing the earlier idea of 'Christendom' in describing a common identity for a community of nations struggling against the divisiveness of religious conflict (Davies 1997, p. 7). While the idea of Europe acquired new meaning following the end of the Second World War, it did not shed its Christian heritage. This is exemplified in a quotation from one of the architects of European cooperation, Belgian politician Paul-Henri Spaak in 1954: 'Do you really need me to remind you that if you sometimes think differently, you all pray in the same way? ... We are members of the same civilisation, known as Christian Civilisation' (Tank 2000, p. 167).

The discourse of exclusion is alive and well within the EU today and considerable sectors of European society continue to claim that Christianity is a basis of identity for Europe. During the framing of the European Constitution, there was a debate on whether Christianity should be incorporated into the text. In the final result, references to Christianity were omitted, despite opposition from the Vatican. This reinforces Turkish suspicions that civilisational factors remain an obstacle to Turkey's membership. Middle East historian Bernard Lewis giving a speech on

---

[12] Indeed, within the Empire, Anatolian Turks did not hold a favorable position as Anatolia was one of the porest and most heavily taxed Ottoman provinces (Østergaard 1997).

Turkish EU membership in November 2003, stated as much, declaring that Turkey cannot become a member of the EU due to its Muslim identity (Lewis 2003). The understanding of the EU as a civilisational bloc persists and defendants of the 'cultural thesis' of a Christian European Union continue to make their voices heard.

However, while Europe's Christian heritage cannot be denied, one cannot ignore the changing cultural complexion of Europe. The devastating bombings of the railway network in Madrid on 11th March 2004, which palpably brought the war on terror to Europe, tragically illustrated the threat posed by disenchanted Muslim communities within the EU. It also fuelled already existing fears in European societies of the 'enemy within', the rise of militant Islam in Europe.[13] This was illustrated by Al Qaeda members who lived and worked in Europe prior to 9/11 and the architects of the Madrid bombings who were North Africans residing in Spain. However, the growth of militant Islam in immigrant communities brought to public attention following the bombings of the London underground in July 2005 and the averted terrorist plot a year later at Heathrow airport is particularly ominous. In both cases, the groups responsible were primarily composed of British-born Muslims. The integration of the ten to fifteen million Muslims residing in the European Union has now become both a cultural, as well as, a security challenge for the EU.

Oliver Roy, a French scholar of Islam, argues that in seeking answers to the phenomenon of radical Islam, one must examine why transnational visions of Islam are more appealing to Muslim immigrants than integration into the European societies to which they belong (Kemp 2004). Leiken (2005, p. 123) offers the following explanation: 'As a consequence of demography, history, ideology, and policy, western Europe now plays host to often disconsolate Muslim offspring, who are its citizens in name but not culturally or socially.' In addressing the issue of militant Islam, the relationship between existing Muslim communities in Europe and their adopted countries, and the ability to foster a sense of belonging to Europe, countering feelings of disenfranchisement and radicalisation, will present both social and security challenges for the EU. Undoubtedly, the persistence of a 'Christian fortress' EU that reinforces perceptions of a civilisational divide can only prove counterproductive in integrating Europe's Muslim communities. So while religion has been utilised in building an identity for Europe, a new European identity accounting for the pluralism of faiths would seem to be in the wider interest of European security. After all, conditions for membership in the EU, the Copenhagen Criteria, are based on secular

---

[13] In a survey of transatlantic trends in 2003, the German Marshall Fund indicated that while Americans and Europeans both perceive the threat of international terrorism at an equal level, Europeans consider the threat of Islamic fundamentalism at a higher level than Americans do (German Marshall Fund and Compagnia di San Paolo, 2003).

norms and values. The AKP, linking the civilisational argument to the security one, therefore argues that Turkey's membership of the EU would send an important signal internally. However, in doing so, the AKP emphasizes Turkey's Muslim identity, much to the discomfort of the secular elite.

This may be a risky policy. While European policymakers recognise the value of the 'Muslim-democratic' model promoted by Turkey, the EU is divided on the acceptance of Muslim Turkey within its ranks. There is a basis for arguing that European identity after the Cold War has been based on an expansion to the East and a containment of the South creating a cultural/religious 'iron curtain' (Yılmaz and Bilgin 2005, p. 270). Examples abound: Valéry Giscard d'Estaing, architect of the European constitution, in 2002 proclaimed an 'end to Europe' if Turkey were to join. In Germany, the Social Democratic government of Gerhard Schröder in 2004 supported Turkey's bid to join the EU, while its rival Christian Democratic Party (CDU) opposed the country's entry based on its size, poor economic record, religious and cultural differences, suggesting instead a 'privileged partnership', a status clearly unacceptable to Turkish policymakers (*Turkish Daily News*, 1st April 2004). Likewise, in France, President Jacques Chirac, reiterating the opinions of his then Foreign Minister Michel Barnier, commented at the end of April 2004 that Turkey was not ready for entry into the EU, making it clear prior to the EU's December 2004 decision that the EU accession process would remain open-ended. In sum, the understanding of the EU as a cultural bloc persists and defendants of the 'cultural thesis' of a Christian European Union continue to make their voices heard. So, while the AKP has made the most progress in bringing Turkey closer to Europe, strengthening the democratic credentials of the party in the process, marketing Turkey's Muslim identity in its approach to Europe might nevertheless backfire.

## The Turkish Military and the EU

Although Turkey may be encouraged by the United States to assume the role of a 'model Muslim democracy' in the 'war on terror' and the EU may be well served with a future Muslim member, acceptance by the Turkish Armed Forces might prove more difficult. The eagerness with which the AKP administration adopts this position serves to compound the suspicions of the secularist military. The question remains whether the Turkish military, the guardians of the secular state, can sanction a reformulation of Turkey's identity and accept the paradox of Turkey's greater usefulness to the West when redefined as part of the East? The Turkish journalist Fikret Bila clearly articulates secular fears concerning the position that Turkey is asked to play in the 'Broader Middle East initiative': 'Which Turkey will be a model in this project

... the democratic and secular Turkey of Atatürk, or a Turkey whose secular and unitary qualities are scrapped and whose religious identity is foremost in its system of government and lifestyle?' (Bila 2004).

When the AKP came to power, there was much speculation as to whether it would be able to continue in power without political intervention by the military. In 1997, an earlier experiment in government by an Islamist party, Welfare [*Refah*], failed when the military pressured the government to resign due to its perceived threat to secularism. Branding Turkey as a model Muslim democracy might prove a dangerous path to tread for the AKP. Fears of intervention by the military in the political process, however subtle, are therefore not entirely unfounded. In particular, the extensive reforms initiated by the AKP in its EU bid have at times strained the relationship between the government and the military. Among other things, these reforms have sought improved rights for Turkish Kurds, a diminished role for the military and a resolution to the Cyprus problem, all issues that the military has traditionally perceived of as critical to national security. The Armed Forces have had to allay public speculation regarding their position by periodically reiterating their commitment to EU membership.

Undoubtedly, the Turkish military are aware that their relationship with the AKP government is a litmus test for the coexistence of democracy and Islam in the Middle East as well as an experiment in Turkey's democratic maturity. Coming to terms with the Ottoman past and Turkey's Islamic identity could increase reconciliation between the secular and the traditionally religious classes in Turkish society, thus strengthening national cohesion. However, for the Westernised elite, including a bulk of the officer corps, the threat of undermining the secular state remains acute and is exacerbated by the suspicion that outside agents are conspiring with Islamists to weaken the Kemalist Republic. The EU's lukewarm acceptance of Turkey serves only to increase their doubts of Europe's intentions.

In assessing the Turkish military's cautious attitude to shifts in identity, it is useful to once again draw upon constructivism-inspired security studies. They suggest that the present symbolic shift in Turkey's geopolitical identity could become a self-fulfilling prophesy if actors 'believe in its truth' (Guzzini 2003, p. 11). Useful though the 'Muslim, democratic' label may be, it does have a powerful resonance in more traditional sectors of Turkish society. Increased demand to express Turkey's Muslim identity through the adoption of Islamic symbols such as the headscarf may be a consequence. This is an issue which continues to cast a shadow over the AKP government. For the military, a shift from the symbolic to the essential suggests a challenge to the identity of the Kemalist Republic which they are committed to protecting. The Armed Forces are likely to perceive essential steps away from Turkey's

Western direction as threats to societal security unless such a move results in binding Turkey closer to Europe. Without a clear commitment to Turkish EU membership which, in their eyes, would secure the country's identity in the West, the stakes are too high for the military. For them, EU membership has a symbolic power in 'fixing' Turkey's identity once and for all as Western, which in turn would release the ideological clamp of Kemalism and allow reforms to proceed.

# Conclusion

Since the establishment of the Republic, the established political elite in Turkey have portrayed Turkey as a secular democracy. They presently face the symbolic redefinition of Turkey by its Western partners who now emphasise its 'Muslim' rather than its 'secular' identity. The shift is all the more difficult given that previously Turkey's Islamic identity earned the country the dubious label of the 'Other', the 'barbarian' repelled at the gates of 'civilisation'. This image of Turkey as the 'Other' was utilised to keep Turkey out of the EU and Turkey's secular elite, in their efforts to further anchor the country in the West, adopted Europe's civilisational demands. Embracing Western culture at the expense of the country's traditional Muslim roots reinforced Turkey's belonging in Europe and continued the construction of Turkey's Western identity as dictated by Kemalist ideology. Writing about Atatürk's thoughts on Westernisation, Berkes notes that Atatürk assumed an 'absolute determination to achieve an unconditional transformation to Western civilisation and to destroy all forces of reaction' (Berkes 1998, p. 464).[14] While it was impossible for Turkey to become Christian, the country could deny its Islamic heritage in an effort to win a place in Western civilisation.

However, after 11th September 2001, Turkey's Islamic identity became a desirable, even 'marketable', attribute and set the stage for an alternative 'branding' of Turkey. The United States' plan to 'democratise' the Middle East stands little chance of success without the support of regional powers while Europe's efforts to create a sense of belonging among its Muslim communities cannot succeed if the EU is perceived as a 'Christian fortress'. Thus, the United States and Europe have begun considering the security advantages, rather than the cultural burdens, of Turkey's Muslim identity. However, much depends on Turkey's ability to keep its reform programme on track and sway European public opinion in its favour. If the Turkish model is to be worthy of emulation, then it must arrive at the same

---

[14] This was a departure from his thinking in the 1870s when he rejected wholeheartedly embracing Western civilisation, in particular its cultural aspects, fearing the gulf that would ensue from 'traditionalist conservatives and imitative Westernists', see Berkes 1998, p. 215.

level of liberal-pluralistic democracy enjoyed in the EU (Oguzlu 2004). Turkey's progress is equally dependent on the continuing incentive of EU membership with the conviction that the EU means to uphold its commitment. Should Turkey succeed, its flexible identity can play an important reconciliatory role in the EU, blurring the 'cultural' boundary and weakening the essentialism of cultural attributes ascribed to East and West. For the secular elite, however, the unintended result will be a reinforcement of the country's ambiguous identity making Turkey no longer simply the 'Other', but ironically, increasingly, the 'necessary Other'.

# Bibliography

Berkes, N., *The Development of Secularism in Turkey* (London: Hurst & Company, 1964, 1998).

Bila, F., 'Hangi Türkiye?' (Author's translation: 'Which Turkey'), *Milliyet daily*, 1 March (2004). Internet: http://milliyet.com.tr/2004/03/01/yazar/bila.html.

Cleveland, W.L., *A History of the Modern Middle East* (Boulder: Westview Press, 1994).

Davies, N., *Europe: A History* (London: Pimlico, 1997).

Deudney, D., 'Geopolitics and Change', in M.W. Doyle and G.J. Ikenberry (eds.), *New Thinking in International Relations Theory* (Boulder: Westview Press, 1997), pp. 91-123.

Fuller, G., 'The Future of Political Islam,' *Foreign Affairs,* vol. 81, no. 2, (2002), pp. 48-60.

Georges-Picot, E., 'Chirac: Turkey Not Fit for Entry into EU', *Washington Post,* 29 April (2004). Internet: http://www.washingtonpost.com/wp-dyn/articles/A53730–2004Apr29.html.

German Marshall Fund and Compagnia di San Paolo, *Transatlantic Trends 2003*. (2003). Internet: www.transatlantictrends.org/apps/gmf/ttweb.nsf

Guzzini, S., 'Self-fulfilling geopolitics?', *Danish Institute for International Studies Working Paper* 23 (2003).

Hale, W., *Turkish Politics and the Military* (London: Routledge, 1994).

Huntington, S., 'The Clash of Civilizations', *Foreign Affairs,* vol. 72, no. 3, (1993), pp. 22-49.

Huntington, S., *The Clash of Civilizations and the Remaking of the World Order* (New York: Simon & Schuster, 1996).

*Hurriyet daily*, 'Powell: Türkiye "İslam cumhuriyeti"' (Author's translation: 'Powell: Turkey is an "Islamic Republic"'), 2 April (2004). Internet: http://www.hurriyetim.com.tr/haber/0,,sid~1@w~3@nvid~392601,00.asp.

Kaplan, L.S., R.W. Clawson and R. Luraghi, *NATO and the Mediterranean* (Delaware: Scholarly Resources Inc, 1985).

Kemp, G., 'Europe's Middle East Challenges', *The Washington Quarterly,* vol. 27, no. 1, (2003), pp. 163-177.

Larrabee, F.S. and I.O. Lesser, *Turkish Foreign Policy in an Age of Uncertainty* (California: Rand publications, 2003).
Internet: http://www.rand.org/publications/MR/MR1612.

Leiken, R.S., 'Europe's Angry Muslims', *Foreign Affairs,* vol. 84, no. 1, (2005), pp. 120-135

Lewis, B., *The Emergence of Modern Turkey* (London: Oxford University Press, 1969).

Lewis, B., 'Turkey in the 21st Century', *Turkey at the Crossroads conference*, American Enterprise Institute, Washington D.C., 22 September (2003).

McGreal, C., 'Turkish PM accuses Israel of practising state terrorism', *The Guardian,* 4 June (2004).

McSweeney, B., *Security, Identity and Interests* (Cambridge: Cambridge University Press, 1999).

Meixler, L., 'Annan Calls on Muslims to Back Iraq Government', *The Guardian*, 14 June (2004).
Internet: //www.guardian.co.uk/worldlatest/story/0,1280,-4203164,00.html.

Oguzlu, H.T., 'Changing Dynamics of Turkey's US and EU relations', *Middle East Policy,* vol. XI, no. 1, (2004), pp. 98-105.

Parla, T., *The Social and Political Thought of Ziya Gökalp 1876-1924* (Leiden: E.J. Brill, 1985).

Powell, C.L., 'The U.S.-Middle East Partnership Initiative: Building Hope for the Years Ahead', Speech given to The Heritage Foundation, Washington D.C., 12 December (2002). Internet: http://www.state.gov/secretary/rm/2002/15920.htm.

Reuber, P., 'Conflict studies and critical geopolitics-theoretical concepts and recent research in political geography', *GeoJournal* 50, (2000), pp. 37-43.

Rustow, D.A., 'Transitions to Democracy', in M. Heper and A. Evin (eds.), *State, Democracy and the Military: Turkey in the 1980s* (Berlin and New York: De Gruyter, 1988).

Sezer, D.B., 'Turkey in the New Security Environment in the Balkan and Black Sea Region', in V. Mastny and R.C. Nation (eds.), *Turkey Between East and West* (Boulder: Westview Press, 1996).

Tank, P., 'A Tidal Europe', in J.P. Burgess and O. Tunander (eds.), *European Security Identities: Contested Understandings of EU and NATO* (Oslo: International Peace Research Institute Report 2/2000), pp. 155-173.

Tank, P., 'Political Islam in Turkey: A State of Controlled Secularity', *Turkish Studies*, vol. 6, no 1, March (2005), pp. 3-19.

Taspınar, Ö., *An Uneven Fit? The 'Turkish' Model and the Arab World*, Analysis Paper No. 5 (Washington DC: The Saban Center for Middle East Policy at the Brookings Institution, 2003).

*The Economist*, 'Bülent Ecevit, Turkey's survivor', 24 April (1999).

*The Guardian*, 'Lack of democracy delays the Arab League', 24 March (2004). Internet: http://www.guardian.co.uk/israel/Story/0,2763,1179999,00.html.

Toprak, B., *Islam and Political Development in Turkey* (Leiden: E.J. Brill, 1981), p.47.

*Turkish Daily News*, 'German party leader optimistic for Turkey's EU prospects', 1 April (2004).

*Turkish Daily News*, 'Erdogan: Despair not Fate for Middle East', 11 June (2004).

*TUSIAD*, 'Selected News on Turkey', Turkish Industrialists' and Businessmen's Association (TUSIAD), Washington Office electronic newsletter, 20 January-2 February (2004).

Vaner, S., 'Turkey and Europe: A Question of Otherness?', *Global Dialogue*, Summer/Autumn (2003), pp. 100-109

van Ham, P., 'The Rise of the Brand State', *Foreign Affairs*, vol. 80, no. 5, (2001), pp. 2-6.

Vick, K., 'U.S.-Turkish Ties Coming Full Circle', *Washington Post*, 27 January (2004).

Wæver, O., B. Buzan, M. Kelstrup and P. Lemaitre, *Identity, Migration and the New Security Agenda in Europe* (London: Pinter, 1993).

Wæver, O., 'European Security Identities 2000', in J.P. Burgess and O. Tunander (eds.), *European Security Identities: Contested Understandings of EU and NATO* (Oslo: International Peace Research Institute Report 2/2000), pp. 29-55.

Yılmaz, E. and P. Bilgin, 'Constructing Turkey's "western" identity during the Cold War', *International Journal*, vol. LXI, no. 1, Winter (2005-2006), pp. 39-59.

Zürcher, E., *Turkey: A Modern History* (London and New York: I.B. Tauris, 1993).

Østergaard, U., 'Nation-States an Empires in the Current Process of European Changes', in O. Tunander, P. Baev and V. Einangel (eds.), *Geopolitics in Post-Wall Europe: Security, Territory and Identity* (London: Sage Publications Ltd, 1997).

# List of Contributors

Brendemoen, Bernt.
> Professor of Turcology, Department of Culture Studies and Oriental Languages, University of Oslo

Iddeng, Jon Wikene.
> Associate professor, Department of Archaeology, Conservation and Historical Studies, University of Oslo

Mønnesland, Svein.
> Professor, Department of Literature, Area Studies and European Languages, University of Oslo

Smilden, Jan-Erik.
> Journalist and master student, Department of Archeology, Conservation and Historical Studies, University of Oslo

Skjelbred, Ann Helene Bolstad, Ph.D.
> Head of Norwegian Ethnological Research, The Norwegian Museum of Cultural History

Soykut, Mustafa.
> Dr. Associate Prof. Middle East Technical University, Department of History, Ankara

Tank, Pınar.
> Research Fellow, International Peace Research Institute, Oslo

Utvik, Bjørn Olav.
> Associate Professor, Department of Culture Studies and Oriental Languages, University of Oslo

# Earlier publications of Tid og Tanke

1. Tor Egil Førland (red.): Norbert Elias:
   En Sosiolog for historikere? (1997)

2. Sølvi Frogner (ed.):
   Fact, fiction and forensic evidence. The potiential of juridical sources for historical research in early period. (1997)

3. Odd Lovoll (red.):
   Migrasjon og tilpasning. Ingrid Semmingsen. Et minneseminar (1998)

4. Hans Jacob Orning, Per Norseng et al (red.):
   Holmgang. Om førmoderne samfunn (2000)

5. Frank Meyer & Jan Eivind Myhre (eds.):
   Nordic Histography in the 20th Century (2000)

6. Jón Viðar Sigurðsson and Preben Meulengracht Sørensen (red.):
   Den nordiske renessansen i høymiddelalderen (2000)

7. Hilde Sandvik, Kari Telste and Gunnar Thorvaldsen (eds.):
   Pathways of the past: Essays in honour of Sølvi Sogner on her 70th anniversary 15. March 2002 (2002)

8. Finn Fuglestad:
   The Ambiguities of History. The Problem of Ethnocentrism in Historical Writing (2005)

9. Kristine Bruland (ed.):
   Essays on Industrialisation in France, Norway and Spain (2005)

10. Iddeng, Jon W. (red.)
    Ad fontes. Antikkvitenskap, kildebehandling og metode (2007)

1–7 are published by and can be ordered from:
IAKH, Universitetet i Oslo
Postboks 1008 Blindern
0315 Oslo
Norway